THINK SPEAK
MANIFEST

ALSO BY KEYIMANI ALFORD

BOOKS

Mile Markers of Life: A 100-Day Christian Devotional for Direction and Strength

Self-Publishing from Scratch: A Practical Guide for Authors to Publish Successfully with Insights for Black Voices

Oakland Hills, Milwaukee Rivers: A Memoir of Survival, Identity, and Purpose

Unshaken Leadership: A Practical Blueprint for Overcoming Challenges, Learning from Mistakes, and Growing in Confidence

AUDIOBOOKS

Oakland Hills, Milwaukee Rivers: A Memoir of Survival, Identity, and Purpose

WORKBOOKS AND JOURNALS

Oakland Hills, Milwaukee Rivers Workbook: A Guide for Faith and Biblical Application

The Healing Companion A Guided Journal for Reflection, Resilience, and Becoming

Unshaken Leadership Workbook: Solve Tough Decisions, Build Trust, and Communicate Clearly in 90 Days

THINK SPEAK MANIFEST

BREAK THE THOUGHT PATTERNS HOLDING YOU BACK AND TAKE CONTROL OF YOUR LIFE

KEYIMANI ALFORD

THINK. SPEAK. MANIFEST.

*Break the Thought Patterns Holding You Back
and Take Control of Your Life.*

Copyright © 2026 by Keyimani L. Alford

All rights reserved. No part of this book may be reproduced, stored in a retrieval system, or transmitted in any form or by any means—electronic, mechanical, photocopying, recording, or otherwise—except for brief quotations in critical articles or reviews, without the prior written permission of the publisher.

Published by Keywords Unlocked Publishers
6969 N. Port Washington Road, Suite B150, PMB #1025
Glendale, Wisconsin 53217

For information about discounts or bulk purchases for educational, church, corporate, or nonprofit use, please email keywordsunlockedllc@gmail.com or visit:
www.keywordsunlocked.com

Cover and Interior Design by Keywords Unlocked, LLC.
Printed in the United States of America.

10 9 8 7 6 5 4 3 2 1

Library of Congress Control Number has been applied for.

ISBN: 979-8-9947595-1-6 (Hardcover)
ISBN: 979-8-9990953-9-8 (Paperback)

To anyone who has wrestled with the voices in your mind—the ones that try to discourage you from becoming all that you were created to be—this book is for you.

May God strengthen every gift, skill, and seed of potential He has placed within your heart, mind, and soul.

ADVANCE PRAISE FOR THINK. SPEAK. MANIFEST.

"*Think. Speak. Manifest.* is a thoughtful and honest book about how high-achievers get stuck under mental pressure, over-responsibility, and performance-based identity, and how to move forward with clarity and relief."

-Advance Reader

"Your story is powerful, emotionally resonant, and highly impactful. The voice is real, grounded, and trustworthy."

- Alexander Harry, Stamford, Connecticut

"The book's strongest asset is clarity of purpose and voice. It speaks directly to overthinkers with lived credibility, and the tools are actionable."

- Ayomide Adewunmi, Lagos, Nigeria

"It speaks with the reader, not at the reader, articulating fear, hesitation, and internal struggle in a way that feels deeply human."

-Advance Reader, Texas

"When the concepts land, they land deeply, offering relief and a reframing of burnout as more than a personal failure."

- Advance Reader

CONTENTS

PREFACE v
    Before You Turn the Page

INTRODUCTION xiii
    Uncovering How to Win the Battle in Your Mind

CHAPTER 1 1
    When Your Mind Hits the Brakes

CHAPTER 2 15
    The Failure Rehearsal

CHAPTER 3 27
    Fear in a Suit: When Caution Feels Like Wisdom

CHAPTER 4 41
    Mental Luggage

CHAPTER 5 53
    Waiting Isn't Wisdom

CHAPTER 6 67
    When Peace Costs You Your Voice

CHAPTER 7 81
    The Timeline Trap

CHAPTER 8 93
    The "Not Ready" Lie

CHAPTER 9 105
Afraid They'll Find Out

CHAPTER 10 119
Catastrophizing Setbacks: When It Feels Like the End

CHAPTER 11 131
When It's All or Nothing

CHAPTER 12 143
The Not-Enough Script

CHAPTER 13 156
When Comfort Betrays Your Growth

CHAPTER 14 169
When "I Got It" Keeps You Alone

CHAPTER 15 181
The Shame Loop

CONCLUSION 197
The Lock and the Key

END NOTES 201

ACKNOWLEDGMENTS 209
My Appreciation to You

THE AUTHOR 211
About Keyimani Alford

PREFACE

Before You Turn the Page

"For as he thinketh in his heart, so is he." —Proverbs 23:7 (KJV)

As humans, I don't think any of us wake up and say, "Today I'm going to give my power away." Most of us start the day with some level of pride, some level of intention, and one simple question: *What do I want to do today?* Sometimes the answer is rest. Other times it's a long list that makes us feel productive. Either way, before we even move, our mind starts forming opinions about what is possible and what is not.

But that kind of power does not only live in our own thoughts. It also lives in the thoughts and opinions of other people. And if we're not careful, we hand them more influence than we ever meant to. This book is about taking that influence back.

It rarely happens in one big moment. It happens in small moments that feel normal. We ask, "How do these look on me?" "Does this sound right?" "Do you think I should do this?" And depending on the response, we adjust our direction. While I've discovered we're smart, I've also seen that we feel safer when certainty comes stamped with someone else's approval.

Look at how quickly we reach for reassurance now. Texts. Group chats. Comments. Reviews. For big decisions and small ones, we often want someone to help us feel sure before we move.

And yes, it can be healthy to lean on people who truly know you. The challenge is when people who don't truly know you start shaping who you think you should be. They form a picture of you, and instead of correcting it, you start living inside it. You shrink to avoid misunderstanding. You stay quiet to keep the peace. You choose what is acceptable instead of what is true. You accept a box that does not fit your values, your morals, your beliefs, or the way you navigate life.

Do that long enough, and one day you realize you don't recognize yourself outside of what everybody expects.

I can say this because it was me.

For a long time, I refused to believe I was giving my power away. I told myself I was in control. But then I started noticing what "control" looked like in my real life. It looked like unspoken rules that came with titles, roles, and affiliations. It looked like being "the leader," "the executive," "the one people count on." It looked like being held to standards that everyone demanded, but not everyone lived. It looked like showing up to everything because of my position, even when showing up pulled me away from what I actually needed to do. It looked like thinking twice before I spoke, not because I didn't have truth to say, but because I knew how fast people could change the way they saw me.

And I'll be honest. It didn't feel good.

As I reflected, searched for answers, and watched what this does to people, I realized how often it shows up in the places we're most connected to: work, religion, friendships, and more. Connection can be life-giving. But people's interpretations can also become a cage.

BEFORE YOU TURN THE PAGE

I've lived in that tension. Loving my impact. Honoring the assignment. Yet still carrying the unfair weight of what people believe someone "in my role" should look like. And once that cycle starts, it becomes easy to live on guard. You monitor yourself, edit yourself, filter yourself, because you don't want backlash. You don't want criticism. You don't want to lose the version of you that people have grown comfortable with.

So you do what many people do. You perform. You carry it with unwarranted pride. You stay busy out of obligation. You stay "strong" for those who are watching you. All the while, you get further away from who you truly are and who you actually want to become. Ironic, right?

Even Superman needs permission to be Clark Kent sometimes.

I need you to listen carefully to what I'm about to say. When you don't decide who has authority in your life, you will start living under voices that were never meant to lead you. Not every opinion deserves a vote. Not every expectation deserves your obedience. Not every person's interpretation deserves to become your identity.

That's why this book exists.

I learned the hard way that what you think influences what you speak, and what you speak becomes the blueprint for what you allow, what you tolerate, and what you manifest. If you keep agreeing with the wrong thoughts, especially thoughts fueled by pressure, fear, and other people's expectations, you will keep building a future that does not match who you really are.

Let me clarify what I mean when I say manifest before we move forward.

Manifest, as I use it in this book, is aligning your thoughts, words, and choices until your life starts reflecting what you truly believe and value. It happens through repeated action, not wishful thinking.

And if any of this sounds like you, you're not alone.

- You overthink simple decisions and feel exhausted before you even start.
- You replay conversations and rewrite what you should've said.
- You feel pressure to be impressive even when nobody asked you to perform.
- You delay because you don't want to be seen learning in real time.
- You keep saying yes, then resent the cost later.
- You keep shrinking to stay safe, but deep down, you're tired of living small.

Now let me tell you one of the biggest lies control tries to sell you. Everybody must approve.

Everybody does not have to approve. Everybody does not have to understand. And they do not get a vote in your timeline. If you don't take control and determine your identity, you will always be vulnerable to getting it from people.

Before you dive into the Introduction, I want you to notice something most people miss.

Other people's opinions do not influence us only because they are loud. They influence us because they often land on something that is already tender. A doubt you already carry. A fear you already wrestle with. A question you have asked yourself in private, even if you have never said it out loud.

That's why this feels like a battle. Your mind is already talking. Measuring. Second-guessing your potential, your worth, your

BEFORE YOU TURN THE PAGE

timing, and your readiness. Then someone else speaks, and suddenly their words don't feel like "just an opinion." They feel like confirmation. Like evidence. And now you're not only fighting what they said, you're fighting what their words woke up inside of you.

This is where control gets dangerous.

It convinces you that you're being wise when you're really being ruled. It convinces you that you're being humble when you're really shrinking. It convinces you that you're being responsible when you're really postponing your future. And once those thoughts take root, they keep growing.

Wouldn't it be liberating if you could recognize it when it shows up and develop strategies to confront it at its core? Imagine the freedom. Imagine the impact. Imagine what it would unlock in your life and your future.

But to get there, we have to go deeper. We have to confront the real issue: what's happening in your mind, and how to win that fight. That starts by identifying where control has been showing up. That's why I want you to take a Control Test, to expose what's been influencing you. Because what you can see clearly, you can finally confront. Answer each question below honestly.

Think. Speak. Manifest.

THE CONTROL TEST

Question	Yes	No
Do you change decisions based on how you think others will react, even when it costs you peace?	☐	☐
Do you replay conversations in your head, wondering if you said the wrong thing or came across the wrong way?	☐	☐
Do other people's opinions linger in your mind long after the moment is over?	☐	☐
Do you hesitate to move forward because you're waiting for validation, permission, or approval?	☐	☐
Have you abandoned a goal because you didn't want the backlash of breaking the mold?	☐	☐
Do you feel pressure to live up to a title, a role, or an image, even when it doesn't allow you to be human?	☐	☐
Do you stay quiet about what you really want because you don't want people to see you differently?	☐	☐
Do you feel responsible for managing other people's emotions, expectations, or reactions?	☐	☐
When you think about stepping fully into purpose, does fear immediately start listing reasons you shouldn't?	☐	☐
Do you sometimes feel like your life is being reacted to instead of directed?	☐	☐

BEFORE YOU TURN THE PAGE

A QUICK REFLECTION

The test was not a pass or fail. It was a moment of honesty. Read each statement and mark Yes or No. Don't overthink it. Don't justify it. Just notice what's true right now.

If you answered Yes to several of these, it doesn't mean you're broken. It means you've become aware of something that has been influencing your thinking, and awareness is where change begins.

Your thoughts shape what you say.
What you say shapes what you allow.
And what you allow shapes what you manifest.

The good news is this: awareness is the beginning of control. And control starts returning the moment you tell the truth about what has been running your mind.

How to Move Forward

This book is designed to be read in order. Each chapter builds on the last, helping you first recognize patterns, then challenge them, and finally replace them with intentional action.

You don't need to rush. Pause when something hits. Write when prompted. Practice what's offered before moving on.

Awareness is not your final destination. It's your starting line.

The pages ahead will guide you step by step out of mental noise and into clarity, so you can move forward with purpose, without carrying the weight of everyone else's voice.

Now let me take you back to a moment where I had to confront what was really controlling my mind.

"For as he thinketh in his heart, so is he."

—Proverbs 23:7 (KJV)

INTRODUCTION

Uncovering How to Win the Battle in Your Mind

"The potential of our future is always connected to our thoughts. What you believe is what you become."

Picture this. You're on a work trip, sitting in a hotel room. Not the fancy kind. Just good enough for sleep, clean enough to relax, and quiet in a way that makes you hear your own thoughts louder. The lights are low, the air is cool, and everything feels still. One of those moments where the world finally slows down... and your mind decides it's time to speak.

It says to you:

What if you fail?

What if you're not ready?

What if you don't have what it takes?

What if you step out and look foolish?

What if you do everything right and it still doesn't work?

You sit there and ponder and ask yourself, "Where is all of this coming from?" Then you realize it's your mind trying to sabotage your future.

That was me, and it often became a cycle I found myself in. And the funny thing is, I'm not alone. Others have these same kinds

Think. Speak. Manifest.

of thoughts. We try to manage our space by drowning out the noise, but sometimes the thoughts in our head are louder than the things around us.

In that hotel room, I had the TV on in the background. I did it more than I'd like to admit. Because when it got too quiet, my mind wandered. And sometimes it didn't wander toward peace. Sometimes it wandered toward the very things I tried not to feel. And that's where this story begins.

While that night was a reflective point for me, reading this might have surfaced your own.

A point where you are thinking about life. About the things that you still want to accomplish. The kind of impact you know you're capable of making. The version of yourself that you see so clearly that it almost feels like you've already met them. But right behind it comes resistance.

You may or may not have an exhaustive list of questions like I had, but you may have thoughts lining up one after another, sounding reasonable, even responsible, yet somehow leaving you feeling smaller instead of motivated. Because that's what it's like when your mind won't let you move forward. You can be sitting still, calm on the outside, and still be battling for your future on the inside.

While reading this, let me share a valuable lesson from one of my favorite movies, *The Avengers*. There is a scene where Bruce Banner is surrounded by chaos, everything pressing in, demanding that the Hulk come out.

But inside Banner, there's resistance. He talks to himself, almost pleading, "Come out, Hulk."

And from somewhere deep within, the answer comes back: no.

UNCOVERING HOW TO WIN THE BATTLE IN YOUR MIND

Inside, the Hulk has the strength. He's got the power. He's got what everybody in that moment needs, but he won't step forward. The outside feels chaotic, exposed, and unpredictable. So he stays inside, locked behind fear and control, waiting until it feels safe enough to emerge.

And I remember thinking, that's what this battle is like.

Because sometimes the strongest part of you, the bold part, the disciplined part, the purpose-driven part, is still inside. It's there, but it's guarded. It's been conditioned to wait. To hesitate. To stay hidden until everything feels certain.

Have you ever felt that in yourself?

I have.

I've second-guessed myself more times than I can count. I've talked myself out of opportunities I prayed for. I've created mental barriers that contradicted the very things I said I wanted. And the truth is, the dream wasn't impossible—it just felt big. It felt risky. It felt like if I stepped out and it didn't work, I'd have to face disappointment out loud.

Fear showed up, sounding helpful. Logical. Protective. And before I ever gave myself a real chance to believe, I was already negotiating myself out of it.

That's when I realized something had to change.

Because we can't keep self-sabotaging ourselves. And research backs up what many of us experience. One major analysis described procrastination as a form of self-regulatory failure, and it defined it as choosing to delay an intended action even when you already expect the delay will make things worse.[1]

I've found self-sabotage doesn't always look like destruction. Sometimes it looks like delay. Sometimes it looks like perfectionism. Sometimes it looks like "I'm just waiting for the right time." Sometimes it looks like staying busy doing good things, so you never have to do the thing that's actually yours.

And often, we don't even admit we're the one doing it.

And that's exactly why I had to develop a tool for myself. Not a theory. Not a motivational quote. A repeatable way to respond when my mind starts spiraling and fear starts dressing itself up as wisdom.

I call it the *TSM Loop.*

And I'm going to share it with you because transformation doesn't happen just because you read something that sounds good. It happens when you learn how to respond in real time.

WHAT IS THE TSM LOOP?

I don't believe we lose momentum because we lack potential. We lose momentum because we don't know how to interrupt what's happening in our mind. And if you don't have a response pattern, you default to whatever feels safest in the moment. The TSM Loop gives you a response. It gives you a way to confront the thought instead of negotiating with it. It gives you a way to move, even when you don't feel ready.

Instead of allowing your mind to continue to sabotage and control your thinking, you'll have a simple tool to change the way you respond to it.

Here's how it works:

THINK: Catch it.

Catch the thought before it catches you.

- *What am I telling myself right now?*

- *What story am I rehearsing?*
- *What outcome am I already assuming?*

SPEAK: Challenge it.

Challenge the thought with truth, not feelings.

- *Is this fact, or is this fear?*
- *Is this wisdom, or is this control?*
- *What is the truth I need to say, even if I don't feel it yet?*

MANIFEST: Commit.

Commit to one measurable step that aligns with truth. Not the whole staircase. One step.

- *What does "done" look like?*
- *What is the next action I can take in the next 10 minutes, the next hour, or the next day?*

Let me show you what that looks like:

Catch it: "If I start and it doesn't work, I'll look foolish."

Challenge it: "That's fear trying to protect my image. The truth is, growth requires discomfort, and my commitment matters more than my perfection."

Commit: "I'm going to take one step today. I'm going to make the call, write the first page, send the email, submit the application, or start the plan."

Think. Speak. Manifest.

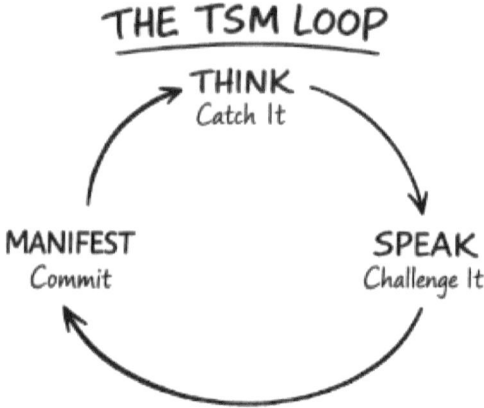

You're going to see this loop throughout the book. Sometimes I'll call it out directly. Other times, you'll notice it in the exercises. But I want you to keep coming back to it, because this is how you stop waiting on a feeling and start building a life.

THE MIND'S JOB: PROTECTION, NOT PURPOSE

Our minds are designed to protect us. They want comfort. Familiarity. Predictability. And I understand that. Familiar feels safe. Familiar feels controlled. Familiar feels like you won't get embarrassed.

But I don't believe our lives were meant to be lived inside the boundaries of what feels safe all the time.

I believe we were created to stretch. To grow. To risk. To become. That's when another realization settled in: dreams aren't random. Dreams are glimpses.

They're not full blueprints, and they don't reveal every step. But dreams give us a window—a picture of what *could* be possible if we stop talking ourselves out of what Heaven is trying to walk us into.

And that's why this book starts with the mind.

Because everything starts there.

Not in your bank account. Not in your connections. Not in your resources. Not even in your talent.

It starts in your mind, because your mind is the place where purpose is either agreed with—or argued with. I've watched too many people, including myself at times, become stagnant not because opportunity didn't exist, but because the battle in their head never got resolved.

The mind is powerful. It's where faith is formed. It's where courage is decided. It's where we either align with what God says—or lean into what fear suggests.

And that's where I had to get honest.

I've spent time caring too much about opinions. Letting other people's perspectives shape my decisions. Giving weight to what family thinks, what friends think, what coworkers think, what critics think, what supporters think. Opinions shift. They change. They can be sincere and still be wrong.

That's when I realized I had been letting opinions—mine and everybody else's—carry too much weight.

And I had to make a decision: am I going to live from fear, or am I going to live from truth? And this is the same question I am going to ask you.

Because your thoughts aren't harmless. They build. They shape what you believe you deserve, what you believe you're capable of, and what you believe is possible. And long before you ever step into purpose, your mind decides whether you'll move forward—or stay contained.

This book is your ammunition to win the battle of your mind. To help you unlock what God placed in you.

Because until we overcome our mind, we'll keep living beneath our purpose. We'll keep delaying what we were born to manifest. We'll keep speaking against our own future—not always out loud, but in the quiet agreements we make with fear.

This isn't a book you read and forget. It's a book you work.

Grab your pen and paper now—because if you commit to what I share in this book, you'll confront patterns you've normalized, break agreements you didn't realize you made, and replace them with truth. You'll learn how to recognize the thought before it becomes a stronghold, how to speak with intention instead of insecurity, and how to move in alignment until your life reflects what you say you believe.

That's why this book is called *Think. Speak. Manifest.*

Because it's time to do the work—to battle what you think so it no longer negatively impacts what you speak, or manifests into your reality.

Let's start where it all begins. The mind.

CHAPTER 1

When Your Mind Hits the Brakes

"Overthinking feels like protection until you realize it's been holding your future hostage."

Right now, someone is calling their overthinking "curiosity." It feels like discovery. It feels like you're processing. It even feels responsible, like you're doing the work to make sense of what happened today. But sometimes that isn't clarity at all. Sometimes it's your mind keeping you busy so you never have to move.

Overthinking has a quiet way of dressing up as progress. Meanwhile, it becomes a lock on the door. It keeps you from stepping into rooms, opportunities, conversations, and risks that could create real impact. And the hardest part is this. You usually don't notice it while it's happening.

I saw it in my own life with writing. I had pieces of chapters, lines that felt like they came from somewhere deeper than inspiration. I had moments that wouldn't leave me alone. Still, I couldn't move. At least, not fully.

Because writing wasn't just writing. It was exposure. Exposure of who I am. Exposure of my flaws. Exposure of what I believed, but also exposure of what I could become. And that was scary.

Think. Speak. Manifest.

My mind kept running the same loop. *If I say this, people will know too much. If I share that, they'll judge me. If I tell the truth, I'll lose control of how I'm seen.* And when you grow up learning how to wear a mask, being seen can feel like danger.

Part of that started in church. Not God, not faith, but the culture around who you're "supposed" to be. What you're allowed to carry in public. What you're allowed to admit. And what you're allowed to heal from out loud. It trains you to measure yourself through other people's eyes. You start editing your life before you even live it.

So I sat on my story.

Four and a half years.

I had things to say, memories to share, and lessons to teach, but I kept weighing every sentence like it might cost me something. It was a battle I was having in my mind and one that I could not seem to win, no matter how much I tried. Have you ever been in a moment where you just felt like you couldn't move forward because of people's opinion of you?

However, something shifted. I reached a point where keeping it in felt heavier than putting it out. I realized the story had value outside of me. It wasn't just my survival. It was somebody else's

> **We sometimes say we don't care, but if we're honest we really do, and it has more merit than we're willing to give it.**

permission slip. And if my purpose was tied to impact, I couldn't keep burying impact under fear.

That was the first version of overthinking I learned to recognize.

And what helped me start breaking that loop was having a response pattern. That's what the TSM Loop is for. Catch it. Challenge it. Commit. Because overthinking doesn't need more attention. It needs a better response.

The second version came dressed as productivity. I brainstorm big visions, and the moment inspiration hits, my mind starts calculating everything it will take. Because I'm often a one-man show, the math gets heavy fast: *I need a team to do X, Y, and Z. Life responsibilities already carry weight.* And the thought becomes, *this is too much to add on.*

Occasionally, my mind swings between ambition and exhaustion. I either isolate and get locked into the work until it strips me from life, or I avoid the work because I'm afraid of what it will take from me.

And then there's a third version: waiting for certainty. I have a book I've sat on because it's a touchy topic and I want the research and framing to be right. I want it to help people. But perfection can become a hiding place, and delay starts calling itself wisdom. This is why the TSM Loop matters. When my mind starts spinning, I don't need more thinking. I need a response pattern. I have to Catch it, Challenge it, and Commit.

WHAT OVERTHINKING ACTUALLY IS

In this chapter, you're going to learn how to Catch what your mind is doing, Challenge what it's telling you, and Commit to movement anyway. Overthinking is when the mind tries to create safety by creating certainty. Psychology describes this pattern in terms of worry and intolerance of uncertainty, where the mind tries to reduce the discomfort of the unknown by mentally preparing for threats, rehearsing outcomes, and attempting to prevent what it fears.[2] It rehearses outcomes, weighs opinions, predicts backlash, calculates workload, and demands perfection before movement is allowed.

It shows up as endless planning, constant research, preemptive defense strategies, or mental rehearsals of conversations that haven't happened yet. It looks productive. It feels responsible. But it keeps you circling the same questions without stepping into answers.

You might recognize it as the voice that says, *I need more time. I need more proof. I need to think this through one more time.* And one more time becomes one hundred more times, and the thing you were meant to do stays locked inside your head.

This isn't the same as thoughtful preparation. Preparation moves you toward action. Overthinking moves you away from risk. And sometimes the only risk is being yourself out loud.

WHY THIS HAPPENS

Now you might be asking the question, where does this come from? I'm glad you asked because overthinking doesn't come from nowhere. It's learned. It grows roots. And if you ignore it long enough, it can crack your foundation like a tree beside a house.

I've got a pine tree on one of my rental properties right now that taught me this lesson in real time. That tree is massive. About 60 feet tall, and thick enough that you have to respect it just standing there. From the outside, it looks strong, stable, even beautiful. The kind of thing you assume has been fine for decades, so it must be safe.

But what you can't see is what's happening underneath.

Those roots went so deep and spread so far that they started lifting the sidewalk like it was nothing. Then the garage foundation cracked. At one point, even the concrete next to the house began to rise. Nothing hit it. There wasn't a storm. It moved because something unseen kept pressing, little by little, day after day, until the structure had to give.

And once that kind of damage shows up, it's never just a "small fix." It costs you time, money, energy, and peace.

That's how overthinking works when it goes unchecked. It can look like wisdom on the surface. It can feel like being careful. It can even convince you that it's helping you stay safe. But underneath, it keeps growing. And if you never deal with the roots, they will eventually push up on the very things you depend on, like your stability, your confidence, your relationships, and your ability to move forward, cracking the foundation you thought would always hold.

And the hardest part is this: you usually don't notice the damage until you see the cracks.

GIVING OVERTHINKING A NAME

I know sometimes it is hard to face the truth, but overthinking can cause real damage in our lives if we don't recognize it for what it is. Let's name the ways those roots usually show up. Overthinking rarely introduces itself as fear. Most of the time, it shows up as protection, and it sounds reasonable until you realize what it is costing you.

Protection from exposure. Trauma can teach you that being seen can lead to harm. If you've been criticized for your truth, shamed for your story, or punished for stepping out of line, your mind builds walls. It decides that invisibility is safer than visibility. When you're about to put something into the world, your brain runs threat assessments. *What will they say? What will they think? What will this cost me?*

Religious conditioning and social masking. Some of us grew up in environments where there was a script for what was acceptable. What you could admit. What you could struggle with. What you could question. And if your real life didn't match the script, you learned to edit yourself and perform. Because being your *true self* would feel like breaking covenant with the version of you people expect.

Opinion sensitivity. When you've been judged before, your mind tries to pre-judge you first. Research on rejection sensitivity shows that prior rejection can prime people to expect it again and become hypervigilant for signs of criticism, even when cues are unclear.[3] It attempts to beat criticism to the punch. Someone gets asked a simple question like, "Are you okay?" and they respond, "I'm always fine." The truth is, they're not fine. They've just learned it feels safer to shut the door before anyone can peek inside. That's a defense mechanism. It forecasts reactions, weighs worst-case scenarios, and convinces you that staying silent is the safest play. You start measuring your purpose against someone else's potential opinion.

Burden and responsibility. Big vision plus limited support makes your brain do the math and hit the brakes. When you can see what something could become but you're also aware of what it will require, the gap between vision and capacity can feel crushing. So you freeze. Or you bounce between all-in and burned out.

All-at-once thinking. Trying to consume the entire thing at once turns progress into pressure. You don't just think about the next chapter. You think about the whole book, the launch, the reviews, the marketing, the long-term impact. And suddenly writing one page feels like climbing a mountain.

Integrity pressure. You care about doing it right. You care about helping people. You care about not causing harm. So you delay to avoid criticism and negative reviews. You tell yourself you're being responsible when sometimes you're just being afraid.

THE COST OF STAYING STUCK

Four and a half years. I can't get that time back. I can tell you what I learned in the wait, but I won't pretend it didn't cost me something.

Have you ever felt stuck? Like you're ready to move, but something in you keeps hitting the brakes? In my case, staying stuck cost me more than time.

I realized the cost showed up in four places—impact, joy, momentum, even my peace. When I think about it more deeply, a message I could've delivered sat undelivered. A hand I could have reached stayed out of reach. While I managed my fear, a moment that could have mattered passed by—and that's a moment I could have regretted.

It also cost me joy. When you're constantly weighing risk and rehearsing criticism, you're not really in the room. You're there, but you're not with yourself. Even in a crowd, it's just you and the loop.

Then there was momentum. I kept restarting in my head without moving in my life. I'd light up, sketch the outline, then talk myself out of it before ink met paper. Inspiration without action becomes its own quiet ache.

And it cost me peace. A mind can't reset while it's running the same drill on repeat—simulations, defenses, bracing for judgments that haven't arrived. That's what overthinking feels like: fear set to autopilot.

Fear always sends an invoice. This is what mine cost.

Overthinking doesn't keep you safe. It keeps you small. And small doesn't protect your purpose. It buries it.

THINK SHIFT: THE TWO-COLUMN TRUTH (CATCH IT)

When your mind starts spinning, you need a way to separate fact from forecast. I call this tool The Two-Column Truth, and it works because it forces your thoughts out of your head and onto paper where you can actually see what you're working with.

Here's how it works. Draw a line down the middle of a blank page. On the left side, write the heading: **What I Know Is True**. On the right side, write: **What I'm Assuming**.

In the left column, list only facts. Things you can prove. Things that have actually happened. In the right column, list everything else: predictions, mind-reading, fear forecasts, worst-case scenarios, imagined opinions.

For example:

What I Know Is True:
1. I have a story worth telling.
2. I've been thinking about this for four years.
3. Writing this could help someone.

What I'm Assuming:

- People will judge me.
- I'll lose control of how I'm seen.
- It won't be good enough.
- Someone will criticize the way I said it.

When you see it like this, you start to notice how much space you've been giving to assumptions. How much power you've been handing to predictions that haven't happened. And you can ask yourself: *am I making decisions based on facts, or am I making decisions based on fear trying to sound intelligent?*

I'll be honest with you: this tool doesn't erase fear. It shrinks it by putting it into perspective, and that gives you room to move forward.

Reflection questions:

1. What part of this is fact, and what part is fear trying to sound intelligent?
2. If nobody could comment on my life, what would I do next?
3. What is the cost of waiting for another year?

SPEAK SHIFT: WHAT YOU REHEARSE, YOU REINFORCE (CHALLENGE IT)

I've learned personally that your internal dialogue shapes your external reality. If you keep telling yourself, *I'm not ready. I need more time. I have to get it perfect first*, those thoughts become agreements. And agreements become actions. Or in this case, inaction.

So we have to change what we rehearse.

Think. Speak. Manifest.

There's a scripture I had to lean on that put this in plain sight for me. Romans 12:2 (KJV) says, "Be not conformed to this world: but be ye transformed by the renewing of your mind…" It reminded me that transformation does not start with my circumstances. It starts with my mind. If my thoughts stay stuck in fear, my feet will stay stuck too.

That verse helped ground me and pull me out of the mental loop. It made me face a hard truth. Some of the things I kept thinking about myself were not "wisdom." They were weights. And I was carrying them like they were normal.

It also became the foundation for how I started reframing my thoughts through affirmations.

As crazy as this sounds, I believe it worked. I did two things.

First, I took a notebook and one Sunday afternoon wrote down what I knew I needed to believe, even if I didn't fully feel it yet: "I am strong." "I am smart." "I am an inspiration to many." "I am a millionaire." (I had to throw that one in there.) I used those statements, and I still do, as reminders. I pull that notebook out each week.

Second, I wrote some of those affirmations on my mirror, the one I look into every day. I'm not doing it because I'm in love with my reflection. I'm doing it because I'm going to stand there anyway. So I decided I should be met with truth instead of doubt.

The examples below will give you an idea of what that can look like, and how you can create your own.

These aren't affirmations you say once and forget. These are truthful redirects. Statements you come back to when your mind tries to lock the door again.

I'm allowed to begin before I feel safe.

WHEN YOUR MIND HITS THE BRAKES

Safety isn't the prerequisite for purpose. Sometimes purpose is what creates safety. You don't wait until the fear is gone. You move with the fear and let the movement teach you that you can handle it.

I can protect my peace without burying my purpose.
Protecting yourself doesn't mean hiding. It means setting boundaries, choosing who gets access, and moving at a pace that honors both your calling and your capacity. You don't have to choose between peace and progress.

I'm not writing to be liked. I'm writing to be honest and helpful.
This one cut through so much noise for me. I had to stop asking *will they like this?* and start asking *is this true? Is this useful?* Likability is not the mission. Impact is.

My responsibility is the work. Their opinion is their work.
You can't control how people receive what you create. You can only control whether you create it with integrity. Their response is between them and whatever they're carrying. Your job is to show up and do the work.

I'm taking the next step, not the whole staircase. This is the one I come back to most often. When my brain tries to map out the entire journey and calculate every possible outcome, I remind myself: I don't need to see the whole staircase. I just need to see the next step. And then I take it.

Speak the Truth (Reframe): What is the truth I need to speak back to my most common overthinking script?

Think. Speak. Manifest.

MANIFEST SHIFT: THE 7-DAY MICRO-PLAN (COMMIT)

Thinking differently and speaking differently won't mean much if you don't move differently. This is where manifestation lives: in the decision to act even when the conditions aren't perfect.

This plan is designed to be small enough that your mind can't talk you out of it, and bold enough that it actually moves you forward.

Small step (today):

Do one small action you've been overthinking, **with zero polishing**.

Send the email. Make the call. Write the first paragraph. Fill out the form. Put the shoes on and walk for 10 minutes. Start the budget. Draft the apology. Whatever your "thing" is, do the first version on purpose.

If you need a prompt, write this at the top of a page or in your notes app: **"What I've been afraid to do is…"** and finish the sentence. Don't edit it. Don't perform. Just be honest. This isn't about a finished product. It's about breaking the seal on hesitation.

Bold step (this week):

Move it **out of your head and into the light**. Tell one trusted person what you're planning to do. Ask someone to hold you accountable. Schedule the appointment. Submit the application. Put it on the calendar and treat it like it matters.

And if you're doing this alone, that's still fine. Record a voice note explaining your next step and why it matters, then listen back.

The point is to turn a loop into a plan and let something outside of your feelings witness it. That's when it gets real.

Consistency habit: I call this **The 20 Minute Move**. Set a timer for 20 minutes. No researching. No scrolling. No "let me watch one more video real quick." No editing. Just forward motion.

Work on the thing. Stop when the timer stops.

This trains your brain that progress doesn't require perfection. It requires presence.

QUICK EXERCISE: THE FEAR UNDERNEATH

This exercise takes 5-10 minutes, and it's designed to surface what's really driving the overthinking. Grab a journal or a notes app and finish these sentences without filtering:

- "If I stop overthinking, I'm afraid that…"
- "The real reason I keep waiting is…"
- "The next honest step I can take is…"
- "If my purpose unfolds over time, my job today is to…"

Don't rush this. Let yourself be honest. Sometimes the fear underneath the overthinking is something tender. Something that makes sense. And when you identify it, it loses some of its power.

WHAT CHANGES WHEN YOU MOVE

When you start applying these shifts, you'll notice some things change faster than others. Here's what to look for.

You start again without needing perfect conditions. You stop waiting for the right mood, the right time, the right level of certainty. You take the next step anyway. And that first step creates a kind of momentum you can't think your way into.

You reduce opinion-based hesitation. You still care about doing things with excellence, but you stop letting imagined criticism run your schedule. You learn how to tell the difference between wisdom and fear. You start moving based on purpose, not pressure.

You produce something concrete. A decision. A boundary. A plan. A conversation you finally had. An application you finally submitted. A walk you finally took. A budget you finally started. Something that exists outside your head. Something real that proves you're not just thinking anymore. You're building.

And your mind gets quieter. Not silent, but quieter. Because you gave your brain action to follow instead of endless scenarios to rehearse. Movement interrupts the loop in a way overthinking never can.

I'm not going to tell you overthinking disappears. I still catch myself calculating risk, forecasting criticism, and trying to map every outcome before I move. But I recognize it faster now, and I know the antidote is not more thinking. It is movement.

Your mind will try to protect you by keeping you still, but stillness is not always safety. Sometimes it is fear with better marketing.

As you move forward, apply these lessons. Take the step. Have the conversation. Send the email. Submit the application. Set the boundary. Start the plan. Write the page if that is your lane. Just move. Because the door only stays locked if you let it.

CHAPTER 2

The Failure Rehearsal

"Sometimes the fear isn't about failure. It's about fallout."

You ever have one of those weeks where you say, "If it isn't one thing, it's another"? That's what it feels like when you start noticing how your mind impacts what you say and what you end up manifesting. Your mind does not surrender. It just gets creative. And with the thousands of thoughts running through us every day, you have to learn how to catch the shift. Because if you don't catch it, you won't challenge it. And if you don't challenge it, you'll never commit to speaking with clarity. That's the loop.

Let's build on what we started. In the last chapter, you learned that action interrupts the loop in ways more thinking never can. You used exercises to separate fact from fear when it tries to sound intelligent.

Now comes the next strategy your mind uses: worst-case thinking. This chapter focuses on fallout fear that edits your truth before you speak. It is harder to catch because it feels like responsibility. It sounds like wisdom. It dresses itself in caution and calls itself preparation. And if you carry any visible role, if people are watching how you move, this pattern will find a home in your head and start decorating.

WHEN TRUTH FEELS LIKE A THREAT

For a long time, my mind treated truth like a threat. It wasn't that I didn't know who I was. I did. The battle was the cost of saying it out loud.

When I finally wrote about my sexuality, it wasn't just a writing decision—it felt like a public decision. I wrestled with the thought that people could take one part of my identity and turn it into a headline about my whole life. I could already feel the different lenses coming toward me: church, leadership, professional, family. And underneath all of it was the same question: *What happens if they find out?*

That worst-case reel started playing before I even finished the thought. *Will people ostracize me? Will colleagues treat me differently? Will this sabotage my career? Will I lose opportunities I worked hard for?* Research on gay, lesbian, and bisexual employees has found that fear about being fully open at work increases when people have experienced or perceive discrimination, and that these fears are linked to psychological strain and career-related outcomes.[4] *Will people assume things that aren't true?*

And some of that fear wasn't imaginary. I've seen reputations get dragged. I've seen one post become the only thing someone remembers about you.

I quickly realized that it was all in my head. Often, people weren't concerned about what I did in my personal life. I, in that moment, amplified the situation because I held onto an insecurity and fear that my authenticity would be judged. When the truth revealed itself, I discovered that many others were open and honest about their sexuality and it felt liberating.

But our mind doesn't always work like that. It sometimes builds a cage out of responsibility. When we're not responsible to anyone except for ourselves.

And that kind of mental rehearsing doesn't just protect you. It can also shrink you. Because when you live in worst-case thinking long enough, you start confusing silence with safety. You start confusing restraint with identity. And one day you wake up realizing you've been managing perception so hard you forgot what freedom feels like.

In real life, most people were not nearly as invested in my personal story as my anxiety assumed. Online was different. Online, people can turn a sentence into a storyline, and that's when truth started feeling like a threat all over again.

The Impact of Social Media

I'm on social media a lot. It's one of my favorite pastimes, but it's also been an eye-opener.

More than once, I've scrolled past a post and thought, Did they really just say that out loud? People will throw out the wildest opinions with zero hesitation. Insults, stereotypes, hot takes, cruel jokes. Then they keep scrolling like nothing happened. No backstory. No accountability. No concern for who might be on the other side of the screen.

And I'll be honest, a part of me used to envy that kind of freedom. Because while other people seemed untouchable, I felt the weight of my seat. Higher education. Public leadership. Church leadership. Fraternity life. Community visibility.

It wasn't just that I cared what people thought. It felt like I had to. Like one wrong sentence could turn into a screenshot, a side conversation, a rumor, or a headline. Like I couldn't be fully human out loud. I rehearsed my words before I ever posted them. Then I watered down what I meant and stayed safe.

And the more I did that, the more I realized silence doesn't just protect you. It shrinks you. I wasn't just editing posts. I was editing myself.

How often do you find yourself doing the same thing? I've done it too, and I didn't even realize what I was practicing. I thought I was being responsible, but I was actually rehearsing disaster. And that's where worst-case thinking starts.

WHAT WORST-CASE THINKING REALLY IS

This is the moment to *Catch* what your mind is forecasting, *Challenge* the script it's rehearsing, and *Commit* to speaking with wisdom instead of fear. If overthinking is the mental loop, worst-case thinking is the loop with consequences attached. It is your mind repeatedly rehearsing the fallout until staying quiet feels like the only responsible option. Clinical psychology describes this as a safety strategy, where people use mental 'safety behaviors' to prevent feared outcomes, like monitoring what they say, rehearsing it, and even avoiding responses because they fear the social cost of being wrong.[5]

You know you are in it when you cannot share an opinion without first running a mental simulation of every possible negative reaction. Workplace research names this pattern self-censorship, the decision to withdraw from speaking, and it often shows up as silence motivated by fear of consequences.[6] When you edit yourself before you speak, not because your words are careless, but because you are already imagining how they will be weaponized. When you rehearse conversations that have not happened yet, preparing defenses for attacks that may never come.

I call this "pre-punishment." Your mind punishes you for something you have not done yet based on outcomes that have not happened yet.

And sometimes it dresses up as discernment. It tells you it is being strategic. Thoughtful. Mature. But underneath, it is fear running the script. Fear that has watched what happens to people who speak up. Fear that knows visibility comes with scrutiny. Fear that is trying to keep you safe by keeping you small.

WHY THIS PATTERN TAKES ROOT

Worst-case thinking does not develop from nowhere. It is built from real observation and lived experience.

Real consequences exist. Your fear is informed by what you have witnessed. You have seen people lose opportunities because of one honest post. You have watched careers shift because someone said the wrong thing at the wrong time. You have seen how quickly a moment of vulnerability can become a permanent mark. So when your mind starts forecasting disaster, it is not pulling from nothing. It is pulling from pattern recognition.

Multiple roles, multiple rules. If you carry leadership in more than one space, you know each space has its own expectations. Higher education has one set of unspoken rules. Church leadership has another. Professional spaces have another. Community visibility has another. And sometimes those rules conflict. So you start calculating how to exist in all those spaces at once without losing ground in any of them. The pressure to manage multiple versions of yourself becomes exhausting.

Think. Speak. Manifest.

Visibility changes the math. When you're in a visible seat, words carry weight beyond intention. You can mean one thing and have it received as 20 different ways. So your mind starts pre-editing in an attempt to avoid what is out of your control.

Masking becomes instinct. If you have spent years learning what is acceptable in each space you occupy, being fully yourself can feel like breaking a covenant. You have trained yourself to adjust, to code-switch, to measure what is safe to reveal. And unlearning that takes more than deciding to be honest. It takes unraveling years of protective instinct.

You are protecting what you built. You worked hard to get where you are. You earned your seat. And the thought of losing it over one misunderstood statement, one vulnerable admission, one moment of unfiltered truth, feels unbearable. So your mind convinces you that silence is preservation.

WHAT STAYING STUCK COSTS YOU

Worst-case thinking steals from you in ways that are hard to measure but impossible to ignore.

It costs you authenticity. You feel edited, even when your heart is honest. You know what you really think, but you are not sure anyone else does. And that gap between who you are and who you let people see starts to widen. You begin to wonder if people would still respect you if they knew the whole truth.

It costs you expression. You silence yourself before you speak. It isn't that you have nothing to say. You've just already mapped out every way it could go wrong. Eventually, you stop trying because the cost of speaking starts to feel higher than the cost of staying silent.

It costs you peace. Your mind stays on patrol. Even in moments that should feel restful, you are scanning. Calculating. Preparing for criticism that has not come yet. That constant vigilance wears you down in ways you do not always notice until you are already exhausted.

It costs you confidence. You doubt your ability to communicate safely. You start second-guessing not just what you say, but whether you should say anything at all. And that doubt does not stay contained to one area. It bleeds into other decisions. Other moments where you could have shown up but chose to stay hidden instead.

It costs you impact. Your voice gets smaller than your calling. You were meant to speak. To lead. To influence. But worst-case thinking convinces you that the safest version of leadership is the quietest one. And the people who needed to hear what you had to say never get the chance.

THINK SHIFT: THE FALLOUT MAP

When your mind starts spiraling into worst-case scenarios, you need a way to interrupt the forecast and get grounded in reality. I call this The Fallout Map. It works because it forces you to name the fear, separate likelihood from catastrophe, and reclaim agency over your choice.

When to use it: The moment you notice yourself rehearsing disaster before you have even acted. When you feel the urge to stay quiet not because of wisdom, but because of a mental movie playing outcomes that have not happened.

How to do it (under 5 minutes):

Step 1: Name the fear in one sentence. Write it down exactly as it feels: "What I am afraid will happen is..." Do not soften it. Do not make it sound more rational than it feels. Just name it.

Step 2: Separate the fallout into three buckets.

Most Likely Outcome	Worst-Case Outcome	Best-Case Outcome
What will probably happen based on evidence, not emotion?	What is the actual disaster scenario your mind keeps playing? Let it be as dramatic as it feels.	What could happen if this goes well? What if people respond with understanding?

Step 3: Ask yourself these questions.

- What part of this is responsibility, and what part is fear trying to control?
- If I chose authenticity with wisdom, what would that look like today?
- What would I regret more: being misunderstood, or never being known?

What it produces: Clarity. A grounded view of what is actually probable versus what your fear keeps rehearsing. Room to choose how you move forward instead of letting fear make the choice for you.

SPEAK SHIFT: THE SCRIPT (CHALLENGE IT)

Your internal dialogue either gives you permission or takes it away. If you keep rehearsing disaster, you will keep choosing silence. Replacing the script helps solve the problem.

THE FAILURE REHEARSAL

I call this practice The Script. Here is how it works: when you catch yourself in worst-case internal dialogue, you swap the line. Not positive affirmations that feel hollow, but honest, grounded statements that tell your mind a different truth.

This is the Challenge step of the TSM Loop. You don't silence the fear. You replace its script.

Old script: "If I say this, everyone will turn on me."
New script: "I can be honest and wise at the same time."

Old script: "I need to stay quiet to stay safe."
New script: "I don't have to be loud to be authentic."

Old script: "One wrong word and everything I built is gone."
New script: "I can speak my truth without surrendering my dignity."

Old script: "Better to stay silent than to be misunderstood."
New script: "I will not let fear write my script."

Old script: "People in my position can't afford to be real."
New script: "I'm allowed to be human, even in a visible seat."

Speak the Truth (Reframe): What sentence do I need to practice until fear stops narrating for me?

Practice these replacements out loud. Write them down. Repeat the one that speaks to your current moment. You don't want to pretend the risk does not exist. However, you do want to stop letting fear have the final word.

MANIFEST SHIFT: THE 7-DAY ACTION LADDER (COMMIT)

Thinking differently and speaking differently will not change your life if you do not practice differently. This plan is designed to move you from rehearsing disaster to practicing honesty with wisdom.

Small step (today): Write a private paragraph titled "The truth I keep editing." No sharing. Just truth. Let yourself say it without running it through every possible reaction first. This is between you and the page.

Bold step (this week): Choose one controlled expression move. Draft a post and run it through a wisdom filter before you share it. Or share a truth with one trusted person who has earned the right to hear it. Or record a two-minute voice note of what you really mean, then rewrite it for public clarity. What you're aiming for is not reckless vulnerability. It is intentional honesty.

Consistency habit (daily): The Wisdom Sentence. Once a day, practice saying one honest sentence in a clean way. Out loud or in writing. No apologies. No disclaimers. Just clarity. This trains you to express truth without catastrophizing the fallout.

QUICK EXERCISE: THE TWO-COLUMN REFRAME

The Two-Column Reframe helps you separate fear from facts. Worst-case thinking works because it feels convincing, especially when it stays in your head. This exercise pulls the thoughts out into the open, slows the mental spiral down, and forces your mind to compare prediction with evidence. By the time you finish, you should have more clarity, less emotional pressure, and one small, wise step you can take without abandoning your values or your responsibilities.

This exercise takes 5-10 minutes to complete and can be done with a journal, piece of paper, or a notes app.

THE FAILURE REHEARSAL

Draw two columns. Label the left column "What My Fear Says Will Happen." Label the right column "What Is More Likely True."

Now, think of something you have been avoiding saying, writing, or doing because of worst-case thinking. In the left column, write every disaster your mind has predicted. Let it be as dramatic as it feels. Write the ostracizing. The career loss. The whispers. The judgment. Get it all out.

In the right column, write what is more likely true. Based on the people actually in your life. Based on what you have seen happen when you have taken measured risks before. Based on evidence, not emotion.

Finish with these three prompts:

- The version of me I protect the most is...
- If I could be fully myself with wisdom, I would...
- The smallest safe step toward authenticity is...

Do not rush this. Let yourself be honest. Sometimes the version of you that you are protecting is not the real you. It is the version you think people need you to be. Naming that gap is the first step toward closing it.

WHAT CHANGES WHEN YOU STOP REHEARSING DISASTER

When you start applying these shifts, you will notice some concrete changes. Not overnight. But over time.

Less mental spiraling before speaking. You will catch yourself starting to rehearse the worst-case scenario, and you will interrupt it faster. You will ask yourself if this is responsibility or fear, and you will make a different choice.

Think. Speak. Manifest.

Clearer boundaries between privacy and shame. You will learn the difference between choosing not to share something because it is personal and choosing not to share something because you are afraid. Privacy is healthy. Shame is isolating. And you will start recognizing which one is driving your silence.

Increased confidence in expressing truth with wisdom. You will stop treating honesty like a threat and start treating it like a tool. You will learn how to say what is real without saying it recklessly. And you will trust yourself to navigate that balance.

One concrete act of honest communication. You will send the text. Post the thought. Have the conversation. Share the truth you have been sitting on. And you will realize the fallout you have been rehearsing did not happen. Or if it did, you handled it.

MOVING FORWARD

I am not going to tell you worst-case thinking disappears. I still catch myself running mental simulations of disaster before I hit publish. I still feel the weight of my seat and the scrutiny that comes with it. But I have learned to separate informed caution from catastrophic forecasting. And I have learned that the cost of silence is often higher than the cost of being misunderstood.

You do not have to choose between authenticity and wisdom. You do not have to be loud to be honest. And you do not have to rehearse every disaster before you are allowed to speak.

Your voice matters. The real one. The one that tells the truth even when your hands shake while you type it.

Write the truth you keep editing. Say the wisdom sentence. Map the fallout and choose anyway. Catch it. Challenge it. Commit.

You are allowed to be human, even in a visible seat.

CHAPTER 3

Fear in a Suit: When Caution Feels Like Wisdom

"Sometimes fear isn't a warning. It's a doorway."

Have you ever had a moment where you didn't do something because it scared you? Pause and think about the real reason. Maybe you questioned if you were ready. Maybe you wondered what people would think. Maybe you felt exposed before you even started.

Those moments can quietly steal time and keep us from making meaningful impact. This is the Catch. Fear rarely introduces itself as fear. It introduces itself as caution. And if you don't catch it early, you'll crown it as wisdom.

There was a season when I realized something that did not feel motivational at all. If I wanted to build my personal brand, and truly deposit into people from my lived experience, I had to be seen. And being seen has a cost when you are used to performing safety. Research backs this up. Studies on disclosure and fear at work show that when people anticipate judgment or consequences, they often manage visibility carefully because the perceived cost feels real, even before anything happens.[7]

Can you imagine how worst-case thinking and the way your mind rehearses disaster can make staying quiet feel like the only responsible option? That's why strategies that help you manage personal perception matter. They help you separate likelihood from catastrophe. Clinical psychology describes worry as a mental attempt to stay braced for what could go wrong. It can feel like responsibility, but it often functions as protection from uncertainty, keeping people rehearsing instead of moving.[8] And when you stop treating every thought like a fact, exercises like The Script introduced in this chapter, become your next move. It replaces fear-driven internal dialogue with honest, grounded statements that actually keep you moving.

But there's a layer underneath all of that. What happens when the fear isn't about getting it wrong, but about being seen in the first place? When the terror isn't failure, but exposure?

That's where this chapter lives. Let me tell you about a recent experience of mine.

THE STAGE

An opportunity came for me to speak on a stage in front of about 700 to 800 people. These were not strangers in a random room. These were colleagues. Friends. People who already had an image of me. People who could compare what they saw to what they expected.

I knew the assignment: encourage, motivate, give people something real to hold onto.

But the moment I pictured myself walking onto that stage, my mind turned into a courtroom.

Are you good enough? Are you skilled enough? Do you have enough notoriety for people to listen? Who do you think you are to stand in front of them? What if you mess up? What if you freeze? What if it falls flat? It all seemed to rise.

I kept telling myself I was being realistic. Preparing for the worst so I would not be caught off guard. But that was not preparation. That was my mind putting me on trial before I had done anything.

The uncertainty made my body feel like it was warning me. The unfamiliar territory made my mind assume it meant danger. And because the fear felt so loud, I almost believed it was telling me to stop.

WHAT I ALMOST MISSED

What I did not recognize at first was that I was treating fear like proof I was not called, when fear is often proof you are stepping into something that matters.

I had to sit with that.

Fear does not always mean you are in the wrong place. Sometimes it means you are in exactly the right place, and your old patterns are fighting to keep you small.

It took time for me to get there mentally, but eventually I did. And when I finally arrived, I had to accept that I did not have to be perfect. I had to trust that alignment matters more than performance. I reminded myself that God does not wait for perfection. He uses willing people.

Eventually, I stepped onto that stage and did what I needed to do. It wasn't flawless, but it was real, and that's why it landed the way it did. When it was over, a colleague messaged me and told me she felt seen. She said it made her think about the impact she makes every day. "And I remember thinking, 'My fear was loud, but it wasn't accurate.'"

That moment taught me something I still carry: fear will try to stop you right at the doorway of your next level.

WHAT THIS TRAP LOOKS LIKE

This is the Think step of the TSM Loop. Before you challenge fear, you have to recognize when it's wearing a suit. This is the trap of confusing fear with a stop sign.

You know you are in it when you feel a pull toward something that matters, but your mind immediately starts issuing objections. When the fear does not just whisper caution but starts acting like a verdict. When you interpret nerves as evidence that you are not ready, not qualified, not enough.

Fear becomes a red light when it is really a moment to check your footing, breathe, and keep moving.

This is different from the worst-case loop we addressed in Chapter 2. That pattern rehearses specific disasters. This pattern questions your right to be in the room at all. It is not about what might go wrong. It is about whether you belong.

WHY THIS HAPPENS

Visibility invites judgment. When you are seen, you are also evaluated. Your mind knows this, and it tries to protect you by convincing you not to step forward in the first place.

Performance pressure distorts the goal. Your mind turns impact into "I must be flawless." Instead of focusing on what you have to offer, you focus on not making mistakes. The assignment becomes survival instead of service.

Familiar audiences intensify self-judgment. Strangers might give you grace. But colleagues, friends, and people who already know you? They can compare. And your mind assumes they will.

Identity questions become accusations. "Who am I to do this?" is not a question. It is shame dressed as a question, and your mind uses it to keep you from answering your own call.

Unfamiliar territory feels like danger. Your body does not always know the difference between "this is new" and "this is a threat." Growth can feel like risk, even when it is not.

When purpose increases, resistance often increases too. I have noticed this pattern in my own life. The closer I get to something that matters, the louder the internal objections become. That is not coincidence. That is friction at the door.

WHAT IT COSTS YOU

When you treat fear as a stop sign, you miss doors you were supposed to walk through. You lose opportunities that would expand your purpose. The stage you do not take, the conversation you do not start, the showing up you avoid. Those moments do not wait forever.

Confidence erodes, because every time you turn back, you reinforce the belief that you were not ready. And that belief compounds. Momentum stalls, because hesitation is not neutral. It trains your mind to pause at every doorway.

Your impact shrinks, because your voice stays trapped behind doubt. The people who needed what you had to say never get to hear it.

Joy gets stolen, because the mind makes the moment feel like threat instead of gift. Even when you finally move, you are bracing instead of present.

THINK SHIFT: THE DOORWAY TEST (CATCH IT)

When fear shows up before a moment that matters, I ask myself one question: Is this fear warning me of danger, or inviting me into growth? Because if I don't catch the fear correctly, I'll mislabel it as wisdom.

That question has saved me more than once. It interrupts the automatic assumption that fear means stop.

When to use it: The moment you feel resistance before something that matters. Before the stage, the post, the pitch, the conversation. When your body is loud and your mind is listing reasons to back out.

How to do it (under 5 minutes):

Grab a piece of paper or open a note on your phone. Draw a line down the middle. On the left, write: **What is truly at risk?** On the right, write: **What is my mind exaggerating?**

On the left side, list the real consequences. Not the feelings. The actual outcomes that could happen. Be honest.

On the right side, list the catastrophes, the embarrassment stories, the "I'm not enough" narratives. Let your mind empty itself.

Then look at both columns. Ask yourself:
- Is this fear about safety, or about being seen?
- If I knew I could not fail in God's hands, what would I do next?

- What does courage look like in one simple step today?

What it produces: You stop guessing and start seeing. And once you see it clearly, you can move.

SPEAK SHIFT: WHAT YOU SAY AT THE DOORWAY (CHALLENGE IT)

The moment before stepping forward is when your internal dialogue matters most. If you let fear write the script, you will talk yourself out of rooms you were meant to enter.

This is where you challenge the verdict fear tries to hand you. Here is what I say to myself now when I feel the old pattern rising:

"I don't need perfection. I need alignment." My job is not to be flawless. My job is to show up in a way that matches what I have been called to do. That is enough.

"Fear can ride with me, but it can't drive." I stopped waiting for fear to leave before I moved. It can be in the car. It just does not get to steer.

"I'm prepared enough to start." I will never feel fully ready. But I know enough to begin. And beginning is where the learning happens.

"My assignment is impact, not applause." I am not performing for approval. I am delivering something I was given to deliver. What people think afterward is not my assignment.

"God can use my willingness more than my polish." This one has carried me further than any technique. Willingness matters more than perfection. I have seen it proven over and over.

Think. Speak. Manifest.

MANIFEST SHIFT: THE 24-HOUR RESET (COMMIT)

You don't need a seven-day plan to move through fear. You sure don't. All you really need is something you can do today to push you forward. This is a same-day reset for moments when fear is loud and the opportunity is close. Because courage doesn't grow in theory. It grows in movement.

Step 1: Name it (5 minutes)

Write one sentence that names the fear. Not the situation. The fear underneath.

Example: "I am afraid that if I mess this up, people will see me as less capable than they thought."

Do not soften it. Do not make it sound reasonable. Just put words to it.

Step 2: Reframe it (5 minutes)

Answer this question in writing: What if this fear is not a wall but a doorway?

Then write one sentence about what is on the other side of this moment if you walk through it. What becomes possible?

Step 3: Move anyway (before the day ends)

Take one action that proves the fear did not win today. It does not have to be the whole thing. It has to be something.

Record a two-minute message as if you are speaking to one person, not a crowd. Save it. Or confirm the opportunity you have been avoiding. Or practice your opening on camera three times, then stop.

What you're aiming for is not to eliminate fear. It's to move before the day ends so that fear does not get the final word.

QUICK EXERCISE: THE FEAR TRACE

The Fear Trace helps you follow fear back to its source. Most of the time, fear is not just about the moment in front of you. It is connected to an old message, a past experience, or a belief you have been carrying for years. This exercise helps you identify what your fear is really built on so you can respond with clarity instead of reacting from reflex.

This takes about 10 minutes. Think of a recent moment when fear stopped you from showing up. Maybe you did not post something. Did not speak up. Did not take the stage or start the conversation. Pick one specific moment.

If your fear isn't about a stage, that counts too—think of any moment you avoided visibility: sending the email, raising your hand, sharing the idea, posting the truth, or setting the boundary.

To help you better understand this strategy for confronting fear in your mind, review the example below to see what your responses could look like after completing the exercise yourself. You're aiming to be honest and analyze your results to support your growth and development. Now fill in four columns represented in the table below:

The Event	The Story I Told Myself	What I Actually Needed	My Next Step
(What happened or almost happened)	(What my fear said about it)	(What would have helped me move)	(What I will do differently next time)

Example:

The Event	The Story I Told Myself	What I Actually Needed	My Next Step
I was invited to speak at a conference but did not confirm	"I'm not ready. People will see through me. I don't have enough credibility yet."	Permission to be imperfect. A reminder that alignment matters more than applause.	Confirm the next opportunity within 48 hours. Practice my opening three times.

Fill in your own version. Be specific. The clarity comes from the details.

WHAT CHANGES WHEN YOU STOP LETTING FEAR DECIDE

Here's what I learned. Fear doesn't disappear, no matter what you do. It just stops being the one in charge. You might still feel it, but you don't let it make the decisions for you anymore.

When you do that, you start stepping forward with less hesitation. Confidence isn't always there, but you've practiced moving even when yours is shaky. You learn what to do when resistance shows up, so it doesn't stop you the way it used to.

And over time, you begin to hear what fear is really saying underneath all that noise. You learn to tell the difference between "this is dangerous" and "this is unfamiliar." Then you stop treating unfamiliar like a verdict.

You complete at least one concrete action. You post the thing. Take the stage. Start the conversation. And you realize that the version of you on the other side of fear is more capable than the version who kept waiting.

You learn that courage and nerves can share the same room. Willingness is enough to start.

LET'S TALK ABOUT IT

I still feel fear before I step into rooms that matter. Sometimes I still hear that courtroom voice—asking who I think I am to stand in front of people. But I've learned something: fear at the doorway isn't a stop sign. It's a signal.

The stage that scared me didn't break me. It built me. And every time I showed up after that, I collected more evidence: I can move even with resistance in my chest.

You don't have to wait until fear gets quiet. You have to learn how to move while it's still loud.

Name the fear. Reframe the doorway. Move before the day ends. The next level isn't behind you. It's on the other side of what you've been avoiding. Walk through it. Catch it. Challenge it. Commit.

SHIFT CHECK

Pause. Reflect. Notice the shift.

Focus: Fear, hesitation, and the stories that stop movement

THINK (Catch It): Patterns I'm Becoming Aware Of

What fear-driven thought keeps showing up when I consider moving forward?

_____

_____

Where have I been hesitating, and what story am I telling myself about why?

_____

_____

SPEAK (Challenge It): Scripts I'm Interrupting

What phrase do I keep repeating to myself that sounds like protection but feels like a cage?

_____

_____

When I hear that inner voice say, "not yet" or "what if," what is it really trying to keep me from?

_____

_____

Speak the Truth (Reframe): What is the truth I need to speak back to that script, even if I don't feel it yet?

The truth is:

_____

_____

MANIFEST (Commit): Evidence of Movement

What is one thing I did this week that I would not have done a month ago?

_____

_____

Where did I feel fear and move anyway, even if the step was small?

_____

_____

MANIFEST (Commit): Recommitment

What am I no longer willing to let fear talk me out of?

_____

_____

What is one decision I will stop postponing this week?

_____

_____

CHAPTER 4

Mental Luggage

"Excellence is good. Carrying everything alone is not."

Would you believe me if I told you that some of the pressure you feel isn't coming from the task in front of you, it's coming from what you think that task will say about you? When your name becomes a verdict, every decision turns into a performance. In this chapter, we're going to separate who you are from what happens, so you can move with clarity instead of fear. And we're going to do it through the TSM Loop: Catch it, Challenge it, Commit. Because pressure doesn't just show up in what you do. It shows up in what you believe your name has to prove.

But there is one thing we have not addressed yet. What happens when the pressure is not about stepping forward, but about never letting anyone down once you do? When the weight you carry is not fear of failure, but fear of your name being attached to anything less than excellent?

This one is personal and can handicap us if we're not careful.

THE PATTERN I DID NOT NAME

This is what happens when you don't catch the pattern early—your yes becomes a reflex instead of a decision. For most of my professional life, I have said yes to things I did not really want to say yes to.

I did it because I cared a lot. I cared about students, the mission, the greater good, and how my name landed in rooms when I wasn't there.

When someone needed help, when an association needed support, when a project needed leadership, I often said yes. Even when I did not have the capacity. Even when I knew I was already stretched.

Over time I realized something about myself. My name is personal to me. I do not want it spoken about negatively. I do not want the stigma of, "Keyimani said he would do it, and he didn't deliver."

I believed if I attached my name to something, I felt like it had to be successful. No excuses. No delays. No explanations.

That mindset turned into overperformance.

There were seasons where I worked a rigorous 40-hour week, sometimes 45 or 50 hours, then turned around and poured another 15 to 20 hours into commitments I took on outside of my core job. I did it to keep my word. I did it to protect my reputation. I did it because I did not want to let anybody down.

The part I had to face is this. The sacrifice was always me.

I would be exhausted. Running on fumes. Carrying weight that nobody else could see because I did not want to disappoint people. I did not want to admit I did not have the bandwidth. I did not want to say the words that would have saved me time, energy, and peace.

"You know what y'all, I can't do this."

Even when I wanted to say it, I did not.

WHAT I WAS REALLY PROTECTING

Looking back, I could see what was happening underneath.

I was not just protecting my reputation. I was protecting my sense of self. My name had become so fused with my delivery that any gap between the two felt like a personal failure. Not a scheduling problem. Not a margin issue. A character flaw.

I kept pushing. I kept producing. I kept delivering. And the work looked successful. But it came with a cost. The cost was my wellbeing.

That is what happens when you attach your identity to outcomes. Your results become your reputation, your reputation becomes your worth, and your worth becomes something you feel you have to earn over and over again. Research has a name for this. Psychologists call it contingent self-worth, which is when your sense of value rises and falls based on performance, approval, or outcomes. When your worth is "earned" instead of rooted, every assignment starts feeling like a test of who you are, not just what you're doing. That is why pressure feels personal even when the task is normal.[9]

It looked like excellence from the outside. Inside, it was fear with good grammar.

If any part of this sounds familiar, you are not lazy and you are not weak. You are probably just carrying a quiet belief that your value is tied to what you produce. Let me name what this trap actually is.

Think. Speak. Manifest.

WHAT THIS TRAP ACTUALLY IS

And if you don't name it, you'll keep calling it "excellence" while it quietly becomes exhaustion.. Attaching identity to outcomes is when you believe your value is proven by your performance and your name is only safe when you always deliver. It turns responsibility into pressure, and pressure into exhaustion.

You know you are in it when saying no feels like betrayal. When rest feels like laziness. When the thought of disappointing someone feels heavier than the weight of running yourself into the ground.

This is different from the fear we addressed in Chapter 3. That chapter was about stepping into visibility. This chapter is about what happens once you are visible. Once people expect things from you. Once your name carries weight.

The trap is not ambition. Ambition is healthy. The trap is when your identity gets so tangled with your output that you cannot separate who you are from what you produce.

WHY THIS HAPPENS

Reputation feels like identity. When your name is attached to something, it feels personal. Because it is. You have worked hard to build credibility, and the thought of that credibility being questioned feels like a threat to who you are.

Integrity runs deep. Keeping your word matters to you. It should. But when integrity has no boundaries, it becomes a weapon you use against yourself. You keep your word to everyone except yourself.

Declining feels like letting people down. You have seen what it looks like when someone overpromises and underdelivers. You do not want to be that person. So you overdeliver instead, even when it costs you.

Leadership conditioning trains you to carry. If you have been in leadership for any length of time, you have been trained to be dependable. To show up. To solve problems. And somewhere along the way, dependability became your identity. Now you do not know how to be respected without being exhausted.

Results become proof of worth. When you deliver, you feel valuable. When you cannot deliver, you feel like you are failing. The math is simple, and it is dangerous. Because that math never lets you rest.

WHAT IT COSTS YOU

When you attach your identity to outcomes, the sacrifice is always you.

You burn out. Not all at once, but slowly. You tell yourself you can handle it, and you can, until you cannot. The exhaustion compounds. I have discovered that this is described as a response to chronic, unmanaged stress, and it often shows up as emotional exhaustion, a growing sense of distance or cynicism, and the feeling that your effectiveness is shrinking. So when I say it happens slowly, I mean the drain is gradual, and it keeps draining until your body and mind finally stop cooperating.[10]

The hours you pour into protecting your name are hours you do not pour into building your future. You serve everyone else's mission while yours waits.

You carry resentment you do not want to name. You agree with your mouth and feel bitter in your chest. And because you chose to take it on, you feel like you have no right to complain.

Rest and joy slip away. The work gets done, but you do not feel good about it. You feel relieved it is over. And relief is not the same as fulfillment.

You lose the ability to set healthy boundaries. Because every boundary feels like a betrayal of your name, your word, your character. So you keep agreeing, and your body keeps paying the bill.

THINK SHIFT: THE NAME TEST (CATCH IT)

Before you commit or overextend, I want you to pause and ask yourself three questions. I call this The Name Test.

1. **Am I saying yes because I have room for this, or because I want to protect my image?**
   Be honest. There is a difference between having the bandwidth and having the fear of what people will think if you do not show up. Both might lead to yes, but only one is sustainable.
2. **If this does not go perfectly, will I still respect myself?**
   This question tells you the truth about whether your worth is riding on the result. If your self-respect depends on flawless delivery, you are setting yourself up to be held hostage by your own standards.
   This is where perfectionism gets misunderstood. Research shows it is not high standards that consist of mistakes, the need to avoid disapproval, and the constant internal pressure to prove yourself.[11] That side of perfectionism is strongly linked to burnout, especially exhaustion, which is why this question exposes the real trap.

3. **What would a wise version of me commit to?**
   Not a pressured version of me. Pressure makes decisions that wisdom would not. When you imagine the version of you who is rested, grounded, and clear, what would that person agree to?

When to use it: Before you agree to anything that requires significant time, energy, or visibility. Before you take on another project, another role, another favor. Before you say yes out of reflex.

SPEAK SHIFT: WHAT YOU SAY WHEN THE PRESSURE RISES (CHALLENGE IT)

The language you use with yourself in high-pressure moments either reinforces the trap or begins to break it.

Here is what the stuck version of me used to say:

I said I would do it, so I have to.
I can't let them down.
I can't have my name attached to failure.
I'll figure it out later.
I'll just sacrifice.

Here is what I say now:

My name doesn't need rescuing. My boundaries need honoring. My reputation is not as fragile as my fear makes it seem. And even if someone is disappointed, that disappointment does not define me.

I can keep my word without losing myself.

Integrity includes keeping my word to myself. If I promised more than I had, the honest move is to renegotiate, not to run myself into the ground.

Capacity is wisdom, not weakness.
Knowing my limits is not failure. It is self-awareness. And self-awareness protects my longevity.

A respectful no protects my yes.
Every time I decline something I do not have room for, I protect the quality of what I have already committed to.

I can renegotiate without shame.
Renegotiating a timeline or scope is not failure. It is honesty. And honesty builds more trust than silent struggle.

Speak the Truth (Reframe): What is one sentence I need to say this week to protect my capacity without guilt?

The truth is: _____

MANIFEST SHIFT: THE CAPACITY REVIEW (COMMIT)

This is not a seven-day plan. This is a weekly experiment. One practice, repeated for a week, with a simple way to track what you notice.

The Practice:

Every Friday, take 10 minutes to answer three questions in writing:

1. What did I take on this week?
2. What did it cost me (energy, time, rest, peace)?
3. What needs to change next week?

Do this for four consecutive Fridays. Do not skip it. Do not just think about it. Write it down.

The Scorecard:

At the end of four weeks, review your answers and look for patterns. Use this simple scoring guide:

Pattern	What It Might Mean
I took on more than I had room for every week	My default is overcommitment. I need a stricter filter before agreeing.
The cost was always my rest or peace	I am sacrificing myself to protect my image. That is not sustainable.
I kept saying "I'll renegotiate" but did not	I am avoiding the discomfort of honesty. That avoidance is costing me.
I noticed one area where I could have declined	That is my next boundary to practice.

What it produces: You start seeing what you have been ignoring. And once you see it, you can do something about it.

QUICK EXERCISE: THE BODY CHECK

The Body Check helps you turn vague stress into clear information. When your mind keeps pushing, your body often starts speaking first through tension, fatigue, tightness, and heaviness. This exercise helps you identify what your body is carrying, what that weight is trying to protect you from, and what one decision could reduce the pressure. By the end, you should have one specific adjustment you can make instead of just telling yourself to "push through."

This takes about 10 minutes. It connects what your mind is holding to what your body is carrying.

Most effective when you keep saying "I'm fine" but your body is tense, heavy, or exhausted—and you know you're carrying too much.

Sit somewhere quiet. Close your eyes if that helps. Breathe. Slow down for a minute.

Now pay attention to where you feel tight, heavy, or wound up. Common places: shoulders, jaw, chest, stomach, lower back.

Once you find the spot, stay with it for a moment. Then answer these questions in writing:

1. **Where does the weight sit in my body right now?**
2. **What is it protecting me from?**
   Be honest. It might be protecting you from disappointment, judgment, conflict, or failure.
3. **What would it feel like to set that weight down, even for an hour?**
4. **What is one thing I could release, renegotiate, or decline that would lighten this load?**

Do not rush through this. Your body keeps score even when your mind is still making excuses.

WHAT CHANGES WHEN YOU STOP CARRYING EVERYTHING

When you start practicing this, something shifts.

You communicate at least one boundary. Maybe it is small. Maybe it is just saying, "I don't have room to take that on right now, but I can support in this smaller way." But you say it. And you survive it.

You reduce overcommitment. You catch yourself before you agree to something you do not have margin for. You ask the three questions. And you make a different choice.

You renegotiate at least one task or timeline. You do not just push through. You have an honest conversation. And you realize the world does not end when you ask for more time or less scope.

You feel less shame around declining. The shame does not disappear completely. But it gets quieter. Because you have evidence now that saying no does not destroy your name. It protects your ability to show up well for what matters most.

WHAT WE DO WITH THIS

I still care about my name. I still want to deliver. I still feel the pull to agree when someone needs something, and I know I could help. But I have learned that excellence and exhaustion are not the same thing. And protecting my name at the cost of my wellbeing is not integrity. It is a trap dressed as responsibility.

You do not have to earn your worth by never disappointing anyone, nor do you have to sacrifice yourself to prove your dependability. You can keep your word and keep yourself at the same time. That, my friend, is not weakness. It's wisdom.

And wisdom, over time, protects your name better than burnout ever could.

CHAPTER 5

Waiting Isn't Wisdom

*"Sometimes the next step doesn't come with a map.
It comes with movement."*

Waiting can look like wisdom, especially when you care about doing things the right way. And I respect that. I really do. But there's a difference between pacing yourself and postponing your purpose. We have to face it. There are moments we've been calling "timing" when it's really hesitation, and hesitation dressed up as responsibility still holds you back. This is the TSM Loop in real time. You Catch the hesitation, you Challenge the excuse, and you Commit to the next step—even without the full map.

And I also have to be honest with you. There's another pattern that can sound mature, feel cautious, and still keep you stuck. It's the habit of waiting for clarity before you move, treating uncertainty like a stop sign instead of a condition you can navigate through. That's where your mind becomes the gatekeeper, deciding you need one more sign, one more confirmation, one more round of thinking before you act. And if we don't name it, it will quietly block the very dreams, goals, and aspirations you keep saying you want to manifest.

This chapter is not about rushing or ignoring wisdom. It's about recognizing when "I'm waiting on clarity" is really fear wearing a calm voice. If you've been stalled because you don't have a full map, this is for you. We're going to use movement to *create* clarity. Because clarity is often the reward for movement, not the prerequisite.

THE ASSIGNMENT

We all like clarity. Clear instructions, clear expectations, and clear direction. Most of the time it's not control. It's that we don't want to waste time and end up like a hamster on a wheel, moving hard but going nowhere.

I've seen that pattern in people, and I've lived it too. Running and running, but still stuck in the same place because the path isn't clear and the mind refuses to move without certainty.

That's why Marie's story has always stayed with me.

Marie is a news reporter. Sharp, dependable, and the kind of person who takes pride in delivering work that holds up under pressure. One week, her editor assigned her a story that carried weight. Not just because it mattered to the newsroom, but because it was a chance to prove her value.

The problem was the instructions weren't clear.

It was basically: "There's something developing with X, Y, and Z. I need you to build the story and bring back something strong."

But there was no clean starting point. No confirmed name. No link to a source. No contact to verify the lead. No guidance on what angle mattered most or what outcome the editor was actually expecting.

So Marie did what responsible people do. She started searching. She pulled threads through public records, prior coverage, and half-formed tips. She made calls that went to voicemail. She chased leads that sounded promising until they fizzled out.

After a while, it started to feel like she was searching for a needle in a haystack.

And what made it worse was that she wasn't just trying to find information. She was trying to find certainty. She didn't want to submit something shaky. She didn't want to put her name on a story that couldn't be backed up. She didn't want to walk into the next editorial meeting with "I tried," when the expectation was "I delivered."

So she slowed down.

She started dragging her feet. Procrastinating. And it wasn't because she didn't care, she did, but the assignment felt like a moving target. And the longer she sat in that uncertainty, the heavier it got.

And that response is more common than people admit. A large meta-analysis describes procrastination as a widespread form of self-regulatory failure, and it shows up most when tasks feel unclear, uncomfortable, or risky because delaying gives short-term relief, even while it creates long-term pressure.[12]

That was Marie. Waiting didn't feel like avoidance at first. It felt like responsibility. It felt like, "Let me get one more confirmation." "Let me find one more source." "Let me make sure this is solid."

But days went by. She gathered pieces, but she still couldn't confirm the story the way it had been presented to her. She had information, but not enough clarity to feel confident that it was the right information. And because she wanted to protect her reputation, she waited longer than she should have. Eventually, she realized something: the clarity she wanted wasn't going to arrive on its own.

WHAT MARIE HAD TO LEARN

Marie did what high performers do when they stop waiting for the perfect conditions. She created her own plan. That was her Commit. Not perfect clarity—forward motion.

She scheduled a quick check-in and asked one question that changed everything: *"What does done look like?"*

Not "What do you want me to find?" but "What would make you say this assignment was successful?"

Then she defined the deliverable. She outlined what she could confirm, what she couldn't, and what she needed to verify next. She wrote a first version of the story with clear placeholders for what still needed confirmation, and she used that draft to force clarity out of vagueness.

That's the trap.

When clarity matters to you, waiting can feel responsible. But waiting can also become the delay that keeps you from building momentum. Sometimes clarity does not come first. It comes after you start.

Marie wanted perfect direction before she moved. What she got was enough information to take one step, and the rest revealed itself along the way.

Now, when direction is vague, she asks what "done" looks like, takes one measurable step, and lets progress reveal the next step.

WHAT THIS TRAP ACTUALLY IS

Waiting for clarity before action happens when you treat uncertainty as a reason to pause instead of a reality to navigate.

You know you're in it when you keep researching instead of producing. Like when you send another email asking for clarification instead of delivering a first draft. Or when you feel stuck, but the real issue isn't that you don't know enough. It's that you don't feel comfortable moving without certainty. And when certainty becomes the goal, action starts feeling risky even when the next step is small.

It feels like wisdom. It looks like thoroughness. But it can become avoidance in a suit.

This connects to what we covered in Chapter 4. There, we talked about how your name being tied to outcomes can create pressure. Here, that same pressure shows up differently. Instead of overcommitting, you hesitate. You delay because you're afraid of delivering something that misses the mark, even when nobody ever clearly explained what "done" was supposed to look like.

WHY THIS HAPPENS

You do not want to waste time. Efficiency matters to you. The idea of working hard on something that turns out to be wrong feels like a failure of planning. So you wait, hoping that more information will prevent wasted effort.

You fear underperforming. Getting it wrong feels personal. Especially if you have been criticized before for misunderstanding an assignment, the instinct to wait for clarity becomes a protective reflex.

Gray areas make you uncomfortable. Some people thrive in ambiguity. You might not be one of them. Vague expectations create anxiety, and the natural response is to seek more definition before you act. Psychology calls this **intolerance of**

uncertainty and it shows that when uncertainty feels unbearable, the mind treats "not knowing" like danger. So people respond by seeking more reassurance, more information, or more certainty before they move, not because they are lazy, but because their nervous system is trying to calm itself down first.[13]

Your reputation is on the line. You want your name tied to strong results. When your identity is connected to your output, unclear tasks feel dangerous. You would rather wait than risk attaching your name to something half-formed.

Past experiences taught you to be careful. Maybe you have been burned before. Maybe you delivered something based on unclear instructions and got criticized for it. That memory stays with you, and now you overcompensate by waiting longer than necessary.

If that's you, I want you to know your hesitation makes sense—you're not broken, you're protecting yourself the best way you learned.

You prefer control and predictable outcomes. Uncertainty feels like a loss of control. And when you cannot predict the outcome, it is easier to pause than to step into the unknown.

WHAT IT COSTS YOU

When you wait too long for clarity, the cost is not obvious at first. But it adds up.

You create delays and last-minute pressure. The time you spend waiting is time you could have spent producing. And eventually, the deadline does not move, so you end up rushing what you could have built steadily.

Anxiety increases. The longer you sit in uncertainty, the more your mind fills the gap with worry. Overthinking takes over. You start second-guessing not just the task but yourself.

You miss opportunities. Some doors do not stay open forever. While you are waiting for perfect clarity, someone else moves with what they have. And they get the result you were still preparing for.

Communication with leadership gets strained. If you keep asking for clarity without producing anything, it can look like hesitation or inability. Even if your intent is thoroughness, the perception can be different.

Your confidence in uncertain environments decreases. Every time you freeze in ambiguity, you reinforce the belief that you cannot function without certainty. And that belief limits where you can go.

THINK SHIFT: THE CLARITY LADDER (CATCH IT)

When expectations are unclear, do not freeze. Climb. Why? Well, it's backed by research through implementation intentions called the "if-then" planning method. Studies show when people pre-decide their next action in response to a situation, they are more likely to start, follow through, and keep moving, even when conditions are not perfect. In other words, you do not wait for clarity. You build it by choosing the next rung.[14]

I call this The Clarity Ladder. It is a simple three-step process you can use in under five minutes when you are stuck waiting for direction that may never come.

Step 1: Define what is known.

Write down the facts. What do you actually know about this task, project, or decision? Not what you assume. Not what you fear. What is confirmed?

Step 2: Define what is unknown.

Write down the questions. What information is missing? What would you need to know to feel confident? Be specific. Vague discomfort is hard to solve. Specific questions can be asked and answered.

Step 3: Define a "good enough" deliverable.

Ask yourself: What would a helpful first version look like? Not a perfect version. A useful one. Something that moves the conversation forward and gives people something to respond to.

When to use it: When you have been stuck for more than a day on something unclear. When you catch yourself waiting instead of working. When the path forward feels foggy and your instinct is to pause.

Reflection questions:

1. What is the smallest version of this task I can complete today?
2. What question, if answered, would remove the biggest confusion?
3. If clarity never comes, what decision can I make anyway?

SPEAK SHIFT: WHAT YOU SAY WHEN THE PATH IS UNCLEAR (CHALLENGE IT)

The language you use in uncertain moments either keeps you frozen or gets you moving.

WAITING ISN'T WISDOM

Here is what the stuck version of me used to say:

I can't start until I know exactly what you want.

This isn't clear.

I don't want to waste time.

I might do it wrong.

I'll wait until it makes sense.

Here is what I say now:

I can move with what I have.
I do not need the full picture to take the next step. I can work with partial information and adjust as I learn more.

I can create clarity through action.
Sometimes the only way to understand the task is to start doing it. Movement produces insight that waiting never will.

I'm going to define the next step and confirm it.
Instead of asking for the whole plan, I will propose my interpretation and check if I am on the right track. That is faster than waiting for someone else to spell it out.

Progress will teach me what perfection can't.
A first draft teaches you more than a month of planning. I would rather learn by doing than stay stuck in preparation.

I can deliver a first version and refine it.
Version one does not have to be final. It just has to exist. Refinement comes after movement, not before.

Speak the Truth (Reframe): What truth do I need to speak when my mind says, "Wait until it's clearer"?

The truth is: _____

MANIFEST SHIFT: THE THREE-STEP SHIFT (COMMIT)

This is a quick reset you can use any time you notice yourself freezing in uncertainty. It takes less than 10 minutes and gets you unstuck.

Step 1: Notice

Pause and name what is happening. Say it out loud or write it down: "I am waiting for clarity before I move. I have been stuck on this for [how long]."

Do not judge it. Just notice it.

Step 2: Name

Identify what you are really afraid of. Is it wasting time? Getting it wrong? Being criticized? Looking unprepared?

Write one sentence: "What I'm really afraid of is…"

Naming the fear shrinks it.

Step 3: Next

Choose one action you can take in the next 30 minutes that moves you forward without requiring full clarity. It could be:

- Writing your three biggest questions and sending them
- Creating a rough outline of what you think the deliverable should include
- Producing a messy first draft and labeling it "Version 1 for feedback." Version 1 is not a verdict—it's a learning draft, and you can reuse this approach anytime you get stuck; each time you run it, you get clearer.
- Scheduling a 15-minute check-in to confirm your interpretation

The goal is not to finish. It's to move. Do not try to do all of this at once—pick one next action and let that be enough for today.

QUICK EXERCISE: THE MIND DUMP + SORT

The Mind Dump + Sort helps you get unstuck when your thoughts are louder than the facts. It moves everything out of your head and onto the page so you can see what emotional noise is, what is actually true, and what you can do next.

By the time you finish, you should feel less mentally crowded and more clear about one concrete step that creates momentum, even if the full plan is not clear yet.

This exercise takes about 10 minutes. It helps you separate the noise from what actually matters. Best used when your mind is loud, you feel tempted to quit, and you cannot tell what is real versus what is emotional.

Grab a piece of paper then set a timer for five minutes. Write down everything swirling in your head about the unclear task or decision. Do not organize it. Do not filter it. Just dump it out. The questions, the fears, the assumptions, the half-formed ideas. Get it out of your head and onto the page.

When the timer goes off, stop writing. Now sort what you wrote into three columns:

Noise	Truth	Next Step
Worries, assumptions, fears that are not based on facts	What you actually know to be true	One concrete action you can take

Example:

Noise	Truth	Next Step
"I'm going to look stupid if I get this wrong"	The instructions were vague; that is not my fault	Send three clarifying questions by end of day
"They're going to think I can't handle this"	I have delivered unclear projects before and figured it out	Draft a one-page Version 1 by Thursday
"I should already know what to do"	No one gave me enough information to know	Schedule a 15-minute call to confirm direction

Once you have sorted it, focus only on the "Next Step" column. That is your forward motion.

WHAT CHANGES WHEN YOU STOP WAITING

When you start practicing these shifts, uncertainty stops being a wall. You freeze less in ambiguity. You still prefer clarity. That does not change. But you learn to move without it. And the movement itself often produces the clarity you were waiting for.

Your communication gets sharper. Instead of vague requests for direction, you ask specific questions. Instead of waiting for someone to tell you what to do, you propose an interpretation and check it. That changes how people see you.

You produce at least one draft or first version. Something exists that did not exist before. And that thing, imperfect as it is, moves the conversation forward faster than another week of waiting would have.

Your confidence in uncertain environments grows. You build evidence that you can function without perfect information. And that evidence compounds.

WHERE THIS GETS REAL

Like the story I shared about Marie, I too, still like clarity. I still prefer to know where I am going before I start walking. That is not a flaw. It is a preference.

But I have learned that clarity is not always a prerequisite. Sometimes it is a product. Sometimes the only way to find direction is to take a step and see what the next step reveals.

Waiting can feel like wisdom. But when it keeps you from moving, it is just fear in a responsible outfit.

You do not need the whole map. You need the next step. Define what you know. Name what you do not. Produce something, even if it is rough.

Movement creates clarity. Waiting rarely does.

CHAPTER 6

When Peace Costs You Your Voice

"If you keep choosing peace at your own expense, you will eventually run out of peace."

Are you going to keep letting him do that to you? Those words usually come from someone who loves you enough to say what you've been avoiding, because they can see it. And today, I'm going to be that person who loves you. And if this doesn't fit your situation, keep reading. Another chapter will. You cannot keep moving through life feeling unseen, swallowing what you need to say, and calling it peace. There's a kind of quiet that isn't peace. It's hiding who you are. This is the loop. You Catch the moment you start shrinking, you Challenge the script that tells you silence is safer, and you Commit to speaking with wisdom instead of fear.

I'm going to ask you straight. Are you the one who keeps shrinking, hoping things will change without you having to speak? If you are, let's talk about how to take your voice back with wisdom, and stop carrying what was never yours to hold.

THE PATTERN I CARRIED

For a long time, I carried other people's opinions like they belonged to me. Not just in leadership. Not just at work. Across life. If someone did not approve, it would mess with my confidence. If someone disagreed, I would start adjusting. I thought I was being collaborative. I thought I was being mature. I thought I was being a team player.

But over time I started noticing a pattern.

I would be the one trying to accommodate everyone else. I would be the one trying to compromise. And somehow, I was the one leaving after sacrificing the most. I wasn't wrong. I was just the one most willing to adjust.

Then I started seeing it clearly. People have agendas. People want what they want. And if you do not have boundaries, some people will run right over you to get there.

I wrote about it in Unshaken Leadership because it is real. Workplace politics is not always loud. Sometimes it looks like someone driving a conversation, steering the room, pushing an initiative, and using your silence as permission.

THE MEETING THAT CHANGED SOMETHING

There was a meeting with a colleague who always seemed comfortable saying whatever they thought. They had a way of driving the room toward what they wanted. It was a familiar dance. They speak. The room adjusts. And I was expected to fold.

But that day, something in me shifted.

They shared their perspective, and I disagreed. Out loud. In the meeting.

Not to be contradictory. Not to embarrass them. Not to prove a point. I disagreed because I needed a boundary. I needed to say, "That may be your reality, but it's not mine. And I'm not going to keep shrinking to make your perspective easier to hear."

I do not know what everyone thought after that meeting. And truthfully, for once, I did not need to know.

What mattered was that I walked away knowing I did not abandon myself. I walked out of that meeting feeling steady, not because the room agreed with me, but because I finally agreed with me.

I was not going to let someone run over me anymore. And that moment felt like the beginning of a different kind of leadership. A leadership that included me.

WHAT THIS TRAP ACTUALLY IS

If you don't Catch it, you'll keep calling it "peace" while it quietly becomes self-abandonment.

People-pleasing is when you trade your voice for approval, then call it peace. From a research perspective, this is called self-silencing, it's the habit of shrinking your real thoughts, needs, or disagreement to keep connection and avoid conflict. It tends to feel like maturity on the surface, but underneath it often functions like a relationship survival strategy, one where your belonging gets protected at the expense of your own voice.[15]

Approval-chasing is when you keep editing yourself because being liked feels safer than being honest.

You know you are in it when you leave conversations feeling smaller than when you entered. When you agree with things you do not actually agree with. When you stay silent because speaking up might cost you something, even though staying silent is already costing you everything.

Think. Speak. Manifest.

This is different from collaboration. Collaboration is healthy. It involves give and take. But people-pleasing is mostly give. You bend, and bend, until one day you realize you have moved so far that you do not recognize your own position anymore.

WHY THIS HAPPENS

Other people's opinions feel like a measure of your worth. If someone is unhappy with you, it can feel personal. Crazy, right? The crazier part is this: it's not because they're right. It's because you've been trained to treat approval like evidence that you are doing okay.

Disagreement feels like danger. Somewhere along the way, you learned that conflict is bad. That good people avoid friction. That being easy to work with is a virtue. And so you stay quiet, even when speaking is necessary.

Being "easy to work with" became your identity. You have been rewarded for being flexible, accommodating, or low maintenance. And now that identity feels hard to challenge, because challenging it might cost you the reputation you built.

Power dynamics punish honesty. In professional environments, politics can be real. You have witnessed how people twist words. You may have even seen how speaking up can backfire on a person. So silence starts to feel like strategy, even when it is surrender.

You want to belong. Being accepted feels urgent. Especially if you have ever been on the outside, the pull to fit in can override the pull to be honest. And so you adjust. You accommodate. You shrink.

You have seen what happens when people push back. Fear of repercussions is not irrational. Organizational researchers actually name this pattern employee silence, especially quiescent silence, when people keep the truth to themselves because speaking up feels unsafe. It's a form of self-protection in an environment where you've learned that honesty can come with a price tag.[16] For example, you might have watched others get labeled, sidelined, or quietly punished for being too direct. So you learned to soften your edges, even when your edges were exactly what the room needed.

WHAT IT COSTS YOU

People-pleasing steals from you in ways that do not show up immediately. But they compound.

Self-respect erodes. You leave the room knowing you did not say what you meant. And that gap between what you felt and what you said gets wider over time.

Energy drains. You carry resentment you never named. You replay conversations wondering why you did not speak up. And that weight sits on you long after the meeting ends.

Boundaries dissolve. Your "yes" becomes an invitation to be overused. People learn that you will accommodate, so they keep asking. And because you keep saying yes, the asks keep coming.

Leadership presence weakens. Others learn they can steer you. They learn your silence is available. And that changes how they approach you, how they negotiate with you, how much space they leave for you.

Peace disappears. The peace you were trying to protect was never real. It was a performance. And performing peace while feeling resentment is exhausting. Eventually, you run out of energy to pretend.

THINK SHIFT: THE TABLE TEST (CATCH IT)

Before you agree, bend, or stay silent, I want you to ask yourself three questions. I call this The Table Test.

1. **Am I being asked to collaborate, or am I being pressured to comply?**
   There is a difference. Collaboration invites your input. Compliance expects your surrender. If you feel like you are being steered instead of being consulted, that is information.
2. **If I say yes, what am I teaching people about access to me?**
   Every yes teaches something. Every silence teaches something. If you keep bending, people learn that bending is what you do. And they will keep expecting it.
3. **Will I respect myself after this conversation?**

This is the question that matters most. Forget what they think. Will you be able to look at yourself and feel aligned? If the answer is no, that is your signal to speak.

How to use it (under 5 minutes):

When you feel the pull to accommodate, pause. Write one sentence: "If I'm honest, what I really want to say is…"

Then write a second sentence: "A respectful version of that sounds like…"

That second sentence is what you say. Use it.

When to use it: Before meetings where you know the pressure will be high. After conversations where you feel like you folded.

Any time you catch yourself shrinking and want to understand why.

SPEAK SHIFT: WHAT YOU SAY WHEN THE PRESSURE RISES (CHALLENGE IT)

The language you use in high-pressure moments either keeps you small or helps you stand.

Here is what the stuck version of me used to say:

I don't want to rock the boat.

It's not that serious.

I'll just go along with it.

I don't want them mad at me.

Let me just stay comfortable.

Here is what I say now:

I can be respectful and still be firm.

Kindness and clarity are not opposites. I can disagree without being disagreeable. I can hold my ground without being hostile.

My voice belongs here too.

I was not invited to this room to be silent. I was invited because I have something to contribute. And contributing sometimes means disagreeing.

Collaboration doesn't require my silence.

Real collaboration includes pushback. If the only acceptable response is agreement, that is not collaboration. That is compliance with a friendlier name.

I'm not responsible for managing everyone's comfort.

Their discomfort with my honesty is not my problem to solve. I can be respectful. I cannot guarantee they will like what I say.

I'm choosing clarity over approval.
Approval feels good in the moment. Clarity protects me over time. I would rather be respected than liked. And I would rather be honest than comfortable.

Speak the Truth (Reframe): What is the one sentence I need to say in rooms where I usually disappear?

The truth is: _____

MANIFEST SHIFT: THE BOUNDARY PLAN (COMMIT)

This is not a seven-day experiment. This is a reset for how you show up in rooms where you have been folding too long. And this is not just a personal preference. Assertiveness training has a documented evidence base, and research reviews show it can help people express needs clearly, reduce avoidance, and increase confidence in interpersonal situations. In plain language, practicing your voice on purpose makes your nervous system stop treating honesty like danger.[17]

What Changes:

Starting this week, you will speak one honest opinion in a meeting or conversation where you would normally stay silent. Not combative. Not aggressive. Just honest. Use one of these sentences if you need a script:

- I see it differently, and here's why.
- I'm not aligned with that approach.
- That doesn't work for me.

What Stays:

You will still be kind. You will still be professional. You will still listen before you speak. The goal is not to become difficult. It's to stop disappearing.

What Stops:

You will stop automatically agreeing to avoid friction. You will stop leaving meetings having sacrificed more than anyone else. You will stop treating your silence like a gift when it is actually a loss.

The Pause Practice (daily):

Before responding in any conversation where you feel pressure, pause for two breaths. Ask yourself the three Table Test questions. Then speak.

This is not about winning arguments. It is about leaving rooms knowing you did not abandon yourself.

QUICK EXERCISE: LETTER TO YOUNGER ME

This letter helps you separate who you are from what you learned. People-pleasing is rarely a personality trait. It's usually a strategy you picked up to stay safe, stay liked, or stay out of trouble. When you write to the younger version of you, you stop treating the pattern like a character flaw and start seeing it as a coping skill that has outlived its purpose. That clarity makes it easier to change without shame.

This takes about 10 minutes. It helps you trace the pattern back to where it began.

Think about a younger version of yourself. The one who first learned that being agreeable was safer than being honest. The one who figured out that approval felt better than conflict. The one who started folding before they knew they were folding.

Now write that version of you a short letter. Keep it specific. Keep it kind.

Start with: "I know why you started doing this..."

Include: What you were trying to protect. What you were afraid of. What you thought would happen if you spoke up.

End with: What you know now. What you wish you had known then. What you want to tell them about the version of you who is learning to stand.

This is not about blame. It is about understanding. Once you understand where it started, you can decide where it ends.

WHAT CHANGES WHEN YOU STOP FOLDING

When you start practicing this, something in you settles.

You feel less anxiety about disagreement. You still care what people think, but you stop letting that care control you. You learn that disagreement doesn't have to mean destruction.

You communicate at least one real boundary. Maybe it is small. Maybe it is in a low-stakes conversation. But you say something honest instead of something safe. And you survive it.

You carry less resentment after meetings. The weight you used to carry home, the replaying of what you should have said, starts to lighten. Because you actually said it.

You gain more stability in leadership spaces, and people start to see you differently. It isn't because you became aggressive. It's because you became present. And presence changes how people treat you.

HERE'S THE PIVOT

I still notice the pull to accommodate. I still feel the temptation to stay comfortable at my own expense. That instinct does not disappear overnight. This is what it looks like to commit to clarity.

But I have learned that peace without honesty is not peace. It is a performance. And performances run out of energy eventually.

Your honest perspective belongs in the room, not just your agreeable one. The one that can say, "I see it differently." The one that can hold a boundary without crumbling. The one that knows the difference between collaboration and compliance.

You do not have to choose between being kind and being clear. You can be both. And being both is what real leadership looks like.

Stop trading what you really think for approval. Approval fades. But the respect you build by standing in your truth? That stays.

SHIFT CHECK

Pause. Reflect. Notice the shift.

Focus: People-pleasing, silence, and the cost of peace

THINK (Catch It): Patterns I'm Becoming Aware Of

Whose approval have I been chasing at the expense of my own peace?

_____

_____

Where have I stayed silent to avoid conflict, and what did it cost me?

_____

_____

SPEAK IT (Challenge It): Scripts I'm Interrupting

What do I keep telling myself to justify shrinking for others?

_____

_____

What phrase do I use to talk myself out of saying what I actually mean?

_____

_____

Speak the Truth (Reframe): What is the truth I need to speak back to that script, even if I don't feel it yet?

The truth is:

_____

_____

MANIFEST (Commit): Evidence of Movement

When did I recently choose honesty over harmony, even if it felt uncomfortable?

_____

_____

Where did I set a boundary or speak up when I normally would have stayed quiet?

_____

_____

MANIFEST (Commit): Recommitment

Whose opinion am I ready to stop managing?

_____

_____

CHAPTER 7

The Timeline Trap

*"You can drive in the same direction
and still be in a different lane."*

You call it timing. You call it being responsible. You call it "waiting until things slow down." But if we're honest, you keep pushing the date because you don't want to be seen starting.

If that hit a nerve, good. We're going there. The fight is in your mind, and you have to win it.

This chapter isn't about patience. It's about the deadlines you keep moving because you're afraid to be seen trying. If you keep saying "next month" or "after I fix a few things," this is the pattern we're breaking.

Not by rushing or forcing clarity.

But by telling the truth about what "later" is really costing you.

Because every time you move the deadline, you teach your mind that *your* word doesn't mean much.

And we're done with that. Ready? Let's break the trap. This is the TSM Loop again. Catch the comparison. Challenge the lie. Commit to your lane.

THE QUIET FIGHT

Comparison has been one of the quiet fights in my life. It did not always look obvious. It looked like observation. It looked like motivation. But underneath it was a question that kept coming back.

Why them and not me?

Psychology explains why that question shows up so fast. Social comparison theory says people have a natural drive to evaluate themselves by comparing to others, especially when the standards feel unclear. So when someone else is winning around you, your brain starts using their timeline as a measuring stick, even when it was never meant to be one.[18]

Successful people have surrounded me for years, and I never realized how much it shaped my thinking. There were always people around doing big things. People whose lives seemed to unlock faster than mine. And for a long time, I did not realize something simple that would have saved me a lot of mental weight.

People have their own lanes. Comparison just makes you forget it.

Admitting that sometimes we are traveling in the same direction, but our paths are different, was a tough realization. Because the vehicles we use to get to the destination are different. And when you forget that you start judging your movement by somebody else's route.

WATCHING SOMEONE ELSE WIN

I watched a close friend get his PhD before I did. I watched him land a vice president job before I did. I watched him move through the industry faster than I did. And I could not lie. It hit me.

Not because he did not deserve it. He did.

But my mind still went there.

Why him?

Why does it seem like things are unlocking for him more than they are unlocking for me?

Am I not advanced enough? Not skilled enough? Not smart enough?

Comparison had me looking at his blessings like they were my scoreboard. And I did not realize I was slowing down my own momentum trying to chase somebody else's life. Have you ever been there? A moment where you just wanted to be further along and it felt like everyone else was moving faster than you. I have. And I know I won't be the last.

THE SHIFT

After some time, I realized I had a choice. I could stay in that thinking, or I could shift. And when I shifted, something changed.

I realized I was trying to chase what was not assigned to me. It felt like something unlocked, and I could see how I was stunting my own growth because I kept measuring it against someone else's timeline. Their responsibility was not mine. Their weight was not mine. Their calling was not mine.

And the truth is, somebody is watching me the same way I was watching them.

I did two things to attack my thoughts. I celebrated him without competing. Then I went home and worked on my personal plan instead of working my feelings. Because my purpose is mine. My timing is mine. My life is mine. And that is what I have control of.

WHAT THIS TRAP ACTUALLY IS

Comparison is when you measure your worth and progress using someone else's timeline, resources, and responsibilities.

You know you are in it when someone else's win feels like your loss. When their announcement makes you question your path. When you scroll past their update and suddenly feel like you are losing ground, even though five minutes ago you felt fine.

There are studies on social media that prove heavy exposure can increase upward social comparison, which is linked to lower self-esteem.[19] Other research also found that more Facebook use predicted short-term drops in how people felt and declines in life satisfaction over time, which helps explain why one scroll can shift your mood like that.[20]

It makes you feel behind even when you are moving.

This trap is sneaky because it often disguises itself as inspiration. You tell yourself you are just observing, just staying motivated, just keeping up. But underneath, you are keeping score. And the score always makes you lose.

WHY THIS HAPPENS

You are surrounded by visible success. Being around high achievers can sharpen you, but it can also mess with how you see yourself. When everyone around you is winning, it is easy to forget that their win is not your benchmark.

You misunderstand purpose as a competition. Somewhere along the way, you started treating your calling like a race. But purpose does not work that way. There is no leaderboard. There is only alignment.

You assume spotlight equals fulfillment. What you see is their visibility. What you do not see is their weight. The responsibilities, the pressure, the cost. You compare your behind-the-scenes to their highlight reel, and the math never works in your favor.

You ignore different lanes and different vehicles. Their path is not your path. Their resources are not your resources. Their season is not your season. But comparison erases all of that and pretends you are running the same race.

You tie speed to worth. If it is not happening fast, you assume it is because you are not good enough. But speed is not a verdict. Some things take longer because they are being built to last.

WHAT IT COSTS YOU

Comparison does not just steal joy. It lies about where you actually are.

Discouragement sets in. You start to feel like nothing you do matters because someone else is always ahead. That feeling slows you down, and the slowdown becomes evidence that you were right to feel late.

You undervalue your own growth. The steps you have taken start to look small when you hold them up against someone else's leap. But your steps are still steps. And they still count.

Impatience and pressure build. You start rushing things that need time. You start forcing outcomes that need process. And the pressure makes you miserable even when you are moving forward.

Resentment creeps in. You do not want to feel it, but it is there. A quiet bitterness toward people who have not done anything wrong except succeed in your line of sight.

You chase the wrong blessing. You start wanting what they have instead of building what is yours. And when you finally get it, you realize it was never meant for you in the first place.

THINK SHIFT: THE LANE CHECK (CATCH IT)

When comparison starts pulling your attention sideways, I want you to bring it back with three simple statements. I call this The Lane Check.

Statement 1: My lane is...

Name your assignment right now. Not where you want to be. Where you are. What is the work in front of you? What has been given to you to steward?

Statement 2: Their lane is...

Name what you admire about them without turning it into a measuring stick. Acknowledge their path without making it your standard.

Statement 3: My next mile is...

Name one action for your direction only. Not something inspired by their success. Something true to your own assignment.

When to use it: When you catch yourself scrolling and spiraling. When someone else's announcement sits heavy on you. When you feel behind and need to remember where you actually are.

Reflection questions:
1. What am I assuming their life feels like?
2. What responsibility are they carrying that I am not seeing?
3. What would I do this week if I was not looking sideways?

SPEAK SHIFT: WHAT YOU SAY WHEN COMPARISON GETS LOUD (CHALLENGE IT)

The internal dialogue during comparison is brutal. It moves fast and it lies well.

Here is what the stuck version of me used to say:

They're ahead and I'm behind.
If I were better, it would be happening by now.
What's wrong with me?
They got what I wanted.
I'm running out of time.

Here is what I say now:

My timing is not a verdict on my worth.
Speed does not determine value. Some things take longer because they are being built right.

I can admire without measuring myself.
Their success can be beautiful without being my benchmark. I can celebrate without competing.

My lane has its own blessings.
What is meant for me is coming through my path, not theirs. I do not need their route to reach my destination.

I'm not behind. I'm building.
Behind assumes we are in the same race. We are not. I am constructing something that takes the time it takes.

God didn't call me to compete. He called me to align.
My job is not to beat anyone. My job is to stay faithful to what I have been given.

Speak the Truth (Reframe): What is the one sentence I need to repeat when comparison tries to rush my timeline?

The truth is: _____

MANIFEST SHIFT: THE RISK LADDER (COMMIT)

Comparison often keeps us frozen because we feel too far back to start. This tool helps you move anyway, one rung at a time. This is the Commit step. Not catching up. Just moving.

Small Risk (today):

Unfollow, mute, or limit one comparison trigger for the next seven days. This could be a person, a platform, or a habit. You are not cutting them off forever. You are giving yourself room to focus.

Medium Risk (this week):

Take one action you have been delaying because you felt behind. Apply for the thing. Submit the draft. Send the pitch. Publish the post. Schedule the meeting. Stop waiting until you feel caught up. You will never feel caught up. Move anyway.

Bold Risk (this month):

Commit a few minutes of "lane work" every day for 30 days. This is how habits start forming in real life. Habit research shows that repeating a small behavior daily in a consistent way increases automaticity over time. It does not happen overnight, but repetition creates momentum, and momentum changes how hard starting feels. That's why this time matters. You're training follow-through, not chasing motivation.[21] Lane work means working only on your goal, your project, your purpose. No scrolling. No comparing. Just building.

Track it with a simple check mark each day. At the end of 30 days, you will have evidence that forward motion was always available to you.

QUICK EXERCISE: THE TWO-COLUMN REFRAME

If you've done the Two-Column Reframe earlier, this is the same reset, just aimed at comparison. It puts the lie on paper so you can see it for what it is.

Left column: **Old Story (What Comparison Says)**

Right column: **Truer Story (What I Know When I'm Grounded)**

Choose one specific comparison that has been sitting on you. Write the old story honestly. Then write the truer story you know when you're not spiraling.

Read the right column out loud. Let it land.

Example:

Old Story	Truer Story
He got the promotion I wanted. I must not be good enough.	He earned that. And my path is different. I am building something that takes longer, and that does not mean I am failing.
She has everything figured out. I am a mess.	I am seeing her wins, not her weight. I do not know what she carries. And my movement is still movement.
I should be further by now.	Further than what? I am exactly where my choices and circumstances have led me. And I can still move forward from here.

Once you have filled in both columns, read the right column out loud. Let it land.

WHAT CHANGES WHEN YOU STOP LOOKING SIDEWAYS

When you start practicing this, comparison gets quieter.

You spiral less when others win. Their success stops feeling like your failure. You can celebrate without collapsing. You can admire without abandoning your own path.

You focus more and build more momentum. The energy you used to spend watching others gets redirected into your own work. And that work starts to move.

You take at least one concrete step toward your goal. Not because you feel ready. Not because you feel caught up.

Because you decided that your assignment deserves your attention.

LET'S TALK ABOUT IT

I still notice comparison when it shows up. I still feel the pull when someone in my circle wins something I have been wanting. That instinct does not disappear just because you recognize it.

But I have learned that comparison lies about the race. It pretends we are all running the same one. We are not.

Your path is yours. Your timing is yours. Your purpose is yours. And nobody else's movement can take that from you.

Stop watching their race and run yours. The blessings in your direction are waiting for your attention. You are not behind. You are building. And building takes time.

CHAPTER 8

The "Not Ready" Lie

"Perfection is often fear wearing a nice suit."

Have you ever watched someone play Double Dutch? Two people are turning the ropes, steady and rhythmic, and the person who wants to jump in is standing on the outside rocking back and forth, waiting for the perfect moment. They're trying to time it so the rope doesn't hit them. And sometimes they wait so long that when they finally jump, they get clipped anyway. The rope didn't change, but their hesitation stole their rhythm. That's the TSM Loop in motion. Catch the control. Challenge the script. Commit to release.

That's how perfectionism works. You don't lose momentum all at once. You lose it in tiny negotiations with yourself. One compromise turns into a pattern, and the pattern starts running your life in the background. You think "not yet." You speak delay. And before you realize it, you manifest stagnation while calling it "high standards."

This chapter shines a light on the "small yes" that's been costing you more than you admit, and it gives you a way back to alignment. Because there's a pattern that can look like excellence and still keep you stuck. It's the habit of waiting until something is perfect before you release it. Tweaking instead of trusting. Revising instead of releasing. Calling it quality when it's really control.

However, it's important to know this chapter isn't telling you to leap without preparation. It's exposing how "not ready" becomes a hiding place. If you keep collecting information but not making moves, we're going to turn readiness into something you *build*, not something you wait for.

WHERE IT SHOWED UP

For me, perfectionism did not only show up in writing. It showed up in leadership.

One of my biggest struggles was delegation. For a long time, I did not truly accept what delegation requires. When you delegate, you are not cloning yourself. You are trusting someone else to produce an outcome.

Then I got an assistant, and it exposed me.

I had to guide her, yes. But I also had to accept a hard truth. If I give someone a task, I cannot dictate every detail of how they do it as long as the outcome is right.

That was difficult for me because presentation matters to me. I care about how things land publicly. I care about excellence. So when something came back to me, I would tweak it. It wasn't wrong. It just wasn't perfect in my eyes.

And I had to sit with this.

My perfection was not always about quality. Sometimes it was about control. Sometimes it was about comfort. Sometimes it was about avoiding the feeling that things might represent me in a way I could not manage.

THE REAL ISSUE

That "not ready yet" mindset can slow everything down. It can keep you revising instead of releasing. Research actually connects this to perfectionism. An analysis on procrastination and multidimensional perfectionism found that the fear-based side of perfectionism (the part driven by concern over mistakes and judgment) is reliably associated with procrastination. In other words, the delay is not always about time. Sometimes it's about protecting yourself from the feeling of being imperfect.[22]

You find yourself tweaking instead of trusting, or better yet, controlling instead of building.

I told myself I was protecting the standard. But what I was really protecting was my sense of control. If I touched everything, I could manage every outcome. If I approved every detail, nothing could go out that I had not personally refined.

The problem is that kind of leadership does not scale. That kind of work does not multiply. And that kind of thinking keeps you exhausted while convincing you that you are being excellent.

WHAT THIS TRAP ACTUALLY IS

Perfectionism convinces you that the work must be flawless before it can be shared. It delays progress by making "ready" the requirement for movement.

The shift is learning to release what is ready enough and refine as you go.

But growth doesn't require flawless. It requires forward.

You know you are in it when you keep editing something that is already good enough. When you take back a task you delegated because it was not done your way. When you delay a launch, a post, a conversation, or a decision because it does not feel polished yet. This is different from having high standards. High standards push you toward excellence. Perfectionism keeps you from finishing. One builds. The other stalls. But what if I told you that research backs up the difference you're naming? It found that perfectionism has two common sides: striving and concern.

> **Not ready is often another name for afraid.**

Striving can look like effort and standards. Concern is the fear side, the self-criticism, the threat of being judged, and that is the side most strongly linked with anxiety and depression. That's why perfection can look polished while still functioning like fear.[23] Shocking, right? And there are reasons why this occurs.

WHY THIS HAPPENS

You fear criticism or misrepresentation. If something goes out and it is not perfect, people might judge it. They might judge you. And that judgment feels like a threat to your credibility.

Your identity is tied to excellence. You have built a reputation on quality. On being thorough. On getting it right. And now that identity makes it hard to release anything that does not meet the highest bar, even when the situation does not require it.

Control is how you cope. When things feel uncertain, controlling the details feels safer. Perfectionism becomes a way to manage anxiety. If you can control the output, you can control the outcome. Or at least it feels that way.

You struggle to trust others' methods. Delegation requires letting go. But if you believe your way is the right way, letting go feels like lowering the standard. So you take it back. You redo it. You stay in the middle of everything.

You confuse quality with perfection. Quality means good enough to serve the purpose. Perfection means flawless in every detail. They are not the same. But perfectionism blurs the line and makes you treat every task like it requires your finest work.

WHAT IT COSTS YOU

Perfectionism does not protect your reputation. It delays your impact.

You miss opportunities. The thing you keep refining could have been released weeks ago. The people who needed it are still waiting. And the window does not always stay open.

You burn out. When you do everything yourself because no one else can do it right, you exhaust yourself. And exhaustion is not excellence. It is the cost of refusing to let go. The research shows that burnout is a common outcome of this pattern. A meta-analysis found that perfectionistic concerns, the side fueled by fear of mistakes and fear of evaluation, has a meaningful positive relationship with burnout across work, education, and sport contexts.[24] So when you feel yourself tightening your grip and carrying it all, it isn't just stressful. It's a known pathway to exhaustion.

Resentment builds. You resent the people who cannot meet your standard. You resent the work that keeps piling up. And underneath, you resent yourself for being stuck in a cycle you created.

Your team cannot grow. If you take back every task, no one learns. If you rewrite every deliverable, no one improves. Perfectionism does not raise the bar for others. It just keeps you doing their work.

Nothing scales. You become the bottleneck. Everything has to pass through you. And the very thing you thought was protecting your quality becomes the thing that limits your capacity.

THINK SHIFT: OUTCOME OVER OPTICS (CATCH IT)

Before you tweak something one more time, I want you to ask yourself a simple question: What is the true outcome required, and what is just my preference?

I call this Outcome Over Optics. It separates the necessary from the comfortable.

When to use it: When you are about to revise something for the third time. When you are tempted to take back a task you delegated. When you feel the pull to delay releasing something that is already good enough.

How to do it (under 5 minutes):

Write down the task or deliverable. Then answer three questions:

1. What outcome does this actually need to produce?
2. Does this current version accomplish that outcome?

3. Am I improving it because it needs it, or because I want to feel more in control?

If the answer to question two is yes and the answer to question three is control, release it.

Reflection questions:
1. Is this improvement necessary, or is it comfort?
2. If this went out at 90% good, what would actually happen?
3. What does "excellent enough" look like today?

SPEAK SHIFT: WHAT YOU SAY WHEN PERFECTION PULLS (CHALLENGE IT)

The internal dialogue of perfectionism sounds responsible. It sounds like quality. But it keeps you stuck. Here is what the stuck version of me used to say:

> *It's not ready yet.*
> *I'll just fix this one thing.*
> *No one else can do it the way I need it done.*
> *I can't release it until it's right.*
> *Let me just take another look.*

Here is what I say now:

It doesn't have to be perfect to be powerful.

Impact does not require flawlessness. Some of the most powerful things I have released were not perfect. They were honest. They were timely. And they landed.

I can correct as I go.

Releasing something does not mean I can never touch it again. I can adjust after it is out. But I cannot adjust something that never leaves my hands.

Progress first, polish second.
Movement matters more than perfection. I would rather be in motion with something imperfect than standing still with something I keep refining.

I can trust outcomes without controlling process.
If the outcome is right, the process does not have to be my process. I can let go of how it gets done and focus on whether it got done.

Done teaches me what perfect never will.
Completion produces feedback. Perfection produces delay. I learn more from releasing than from revising.

Speak the Truth (Reframe): What truth do I need to say when perfectionism tells me, "Not yet"?

The truth is: _____

MANIFEST SHIFT: THE DEBRIEF METHOD (COMMIT)

This is not a seven-day plan. This is a practice you can use any time perfectionism has slowed you down. It helps you review what happened, extract the lesson, and choose your next move.

Step 1: Review the moment.

Think about a recent time when perfectionism delayed you. Maybe you rewrote something that was already good. Maybe you took back a task you delegated. Maybe you missed a deadline because you kept refining.

Write one sentence describing what happened.

Step 2: Extract the lesson.

Ask yourself: What was I really protecting? Was it quality, or was it control? Was I improving the work, or was I managing my anxiety?

Write one sentence naming what was underneath the perfectionism.

Step 3: Choose your next move.

Based on what you learned, decide on one concrete action. Maybe it is releasing something at 90%. Maybe it is delegating without taking it back. Maybe it is setting a deadline and honoring it.

Write one sentence stating what you will do differently next time.

Use this method weekly. Every Friday, review one moment where perfectionism showed up. Debrief it. Choose a different move for next week.

QUICK EXERCISE: THE PURPOSE PROOF LIST

Perfectionism has a short memory. It only remembers what still needs fixing, not what has already been finished. This list helps you rebuild evidence. It reminds your mind that progress is real, results still happened, and your life did not fall apart because something was not flawless. By the time you finish, you should feel more grounded and more willing to release what is ready.

You will need 10 minutes to complete this exercise. It is designed to counter perfectionism by showing you what you have already accomplished without being perfect.

Think. Speak. Manifest.

Write five things you have completed, released, or accomplished in the past year. They do not have to be big. They just have to be done.

For each one, answer:

1. Was it perfect when I released it?
2. Did it still accomplish something?
3. What did I learn from finishing it?

Here's what it can look like.

Example:

What I Completed	Was It Perfect?	Did It Accomplish Something?	What I Learned
Launched a workshop	No, the slides had a typo	Yes, 40 people attended and gave positive feedback	People cared about the content, not the typo
Delegated a report	No, I wanted to rewrite it	Yes, it was submitted on time	My assistant's version was good enough
Posted an article	No, I second-guessed the ending	Yes, it started three conversations	Done is better than endlessly revised

Once you have filled in the list, read it back out loud. Let it remind you that imperfect things still produce results, and finished work builds confidence faster than flawless plans.

WHAT CHANGES WHEN YOU RELEASE BEFORE PERFECT

When you practice these shifts, perfectionism starts to loosen because you finally let something leave your hands. You release a deliverable that's "ready enough," and instead of the world falling apart, you get evidence: it does what it was meant to do.

From there, your time and energy begin to come back. You spend less mental bandwidth polishing what doesn't need polishing, and you protect your focus for the work that actually requires your voice. You also learn to trust outcomes over methods—delegating without rewriting, giving clear standards, and letting people deliver in their own style. "Excellent enough" becomes the new standard: not lowering the bar, but building with wisdom so your momentum stays alive..

A Needed Shift

The part about me that still cares about quality and wanting things to land well is not going anywhere. And honestly, it shouldn't. But I have learned that perfectionism is not the same as excellence. Excellence finishes. Perfectionism delays.

You do not have to lower your standards to release your work. You do have to separate what is necessary and trust that done teaches you what perfect never will.

I encourage you to release the thing, delegate the task, and stop tweaking what is already good enough. Progress first. Polish second. And that is how you build.

CHAPTER 9

Afraid They'll Find Out

*"You can earn the room and still feel like
you borrowed the chair."*

Perfectionism is a moving finish line that keeps you running and never arriving.

Perfectionism doesn't always call itself perfectionism. Sometimes it calls itself "high standards," excellence, and "I just want to do it right." And impostor thoughts don't always scream. They whisper, Don't get exposed. This is where the TSM Loop gets practical. Catch the lie. Challenge the whisper. Commit to ownership.

This chapter is about what happens when those voices team up, not to make you better, but to make you smaller. It makes you second-guess your seat at the table, downplay your wins, and stay quiet when it's time to own what you built.

It's the voice that whispers: *You got lucky. They don't really know you. If they saw the whole picture, they wouldn't be impressed.*

Have you ever found yourself shrinking even after you earned the room? If so, let's talk about it, because it happens more than we think. And research backs that up.

A large systematic review found that impostor thoughts show up across many populations, with reported rates ranging widely depending on how they're measured.[25] The same review links impostor experiences to anxiety, depression, burnout, and reduced job satisfaction. So when you feel yourself shrinking, you are not making it up. You're responding to a documented pattern that can quietly shape how people show up in rooms they earned.

THE ROOM FULL OF COLLEAGUES

Impostor thoughts have followed me into rooms I earned. And as a Black man, that feeling can come with a familiar weight. You walk into a space and your mind starts scanning for proof you belong. You notice titles, degrees, positions, confidence. And if you are not careful, you shrink.

I remember being at an all-college assembly after COVID. People were being recognized, updates were being shared, and I was sitting in the middle of it. During that time, I had managed a portfolio of about $31 million in emergency funding.

Not casually. Not on the side.

I helped determine the rules. The administration. The distribution plan. The process to get that money into the hands of 16,000 students. Nuts and bolts. Real impact.

And when it came time to introduce myself and share what I had done, I did not say it.

I sat back. Let others have the spotlight. I acted like I was just following directives, like I did not carry a major part of the work. The president called it out, naming what I had done, almost forcing me to be seen.

And in that moment, I realized something about myself.

I was not being humble. I was hiding. After that, I started practicing saying it out loud. Not to brag, but to tell the truth. Ownership is not arrogance. It's accuracy.

I was trying not to look like I was bragging, but the truth is I was not taking ownership. I was minimizing my contribution because some part of me still did not believe I had the right to stand fully in it.

The thought that kept returning was: *If I say too much, they will think I am showing off. Or worse, they will look closer and see that I am not that impressive.*

That is what impostor thinking does. It makes you act like the work was not yours even when your hands are all over it.

THE MIND TRAP

Impostor thoughts convince you that your success is accidental, temporary, or undeserved, so you shrink to avoid exposure. Because impostor thinking doesn't just attack confidence. It edits your voice.

It is the feeling that you slipped through. That your credentials were a fluke. That if people really knew how uncertain you felt inside, they would lose respect for you. So you preemptively minimize. You downplay. You let someone else take credit for the thing you built because speaking up feels too risky.

I learned this the hard way: impostor syndrome isn't always about confidence. Sometimes it's about identity.

This pattern does not just affect how we feel. It affects how we behave, and it makes us small in moments that were made for us.

Impostor thoughts do not mean you are unqualified. They mean you are visible. And visibility triggers fear when you have not practiced ownership.

So the work is not proving yourself. The work is owning yourself.

WHY THIS HAPPENS

Impostor thinking does not come from nowhere. It often has roots.

Racialized pressure and stereotype threat. Research on stereotype threat shows that when people feel they might be judged through a stereotype, it can trigger stress and vigilance that drains mental resources.[26] That's part of why some people minimize instead of claim. It is not lack of ability. It is the mental tax of being watched and measured differently. When you occupy spaces where people who look like you have been underrepresented, there can be an unspoken weight. You carry your own work plus the pressure of representing something larger. That burden can make you hyper-aware of how you are being perceived, which leads to minimizing rather than claiming.

Fear of being judged as arrogant. We are often taught to be humble. Stay in your place. Do not get too big for your britches. While humility has value, it becomes a trap when it stops you from speaking truthfully about what you have done. Confidence is not arrogance. Arrogance dismisses others. Confidence simply tells the truth about your own contribution.

High-achievement environments that trigger comparison. When smart, accomplished people surround you, your mind can start keeping score. You see what they have and start questioning whether you measure up. Comparison does not just steal joy. It steals accuracy. It makes you see your own work through a distorted lens.

Internalized belief: I must prove it again. Some of us learned early that one success does not secure your place. You have to keep earning it. Keep proving it. Keep defending it. That belief can become exhausting, and it makes every new room feel like another test.

These roots do not make the pattern permanent. They just help explain why it formed. And once you understand the cause, you can challenge the conclusion.

THE COST

When you stay silent about what you have done, someone else will define your narrative.

You miss visibility and advancement opportunities. It isn't that you're not qualified. People simply can't support what they can't see. Promotions, partnerships, and recognition often go to the people who can articulate their impact. If you can't say it, others won't know it.

You lose confidence in leadership spaces. When you constantly second-guess your right to be in the room, you hold back ideas. You speak less. You contribute less. And the room misses what you had to offer.

Your impact goes under-recognized. It wasn't small. You just treated it like it was. And over time, that pattern can erode your own memory of what you've accomplished.

You stay small while doing big work. That is the real cost. Not that you lack ability. You are hiding ability you already have.

THINK SHIFT: EVIDENCE INVENTORY (CATCH IT)

Here is what helped me when impostor thoughts started taking the wheel.

The Tool: Evidence Inventory

Impostor thoughts are not based on facts. They are based on fear. So we counter them with evidence. Cognitive restructuring aligns this practice with psychology. It's where you put the thought on the table and examine it with evidence instead of letting it run your life unchecked. An analysis of cognitive restructuring research connected this kind of evidence-based reframe work to improvements in psychotherapy outcomes, which is why writing the truth down can interrupt a fear script that feels convincing in your head.[27]

When you feel like you do not belong, write down five pieces of evidence that you earned the room. Facts only. Not feelings. Not what you hope is true. What is actually true.

For example:

- I managed a $31 million emergency fund distribution.
- I helped create the rules and process that served 16,000 students.
- I completed the certification required for this role.
- I was invited to this table by someone who saw my work.
- I delivered the project on time, under budget, with measurable results.

When to use it: Before walking into a high-visibility room. After receiving recognition you feel tempted to deflect. When you catch yourself thinking, *I got lucky*.

How long it takes: Less than five minutes. You already know the evidence. You just need to give it language.

What it produces: Grounded confidence. A reminder that you did not slip through. You walked in with something real.

Reflection Questions:
1. If someone else did what I did, what would I call it?
2. Why is it easier to celebrate others than myself?
3. What story am I afraid people will tell if I own my success?

SPEAK SHIFT: THE WORDS I PRACTICE (CHALLENGE IT)

When my mind is loud, my words matter even more. The language I use with myself shapes the posture I bring into the room.

Here are the phrases I stopped saying:

I was just in the right place at the right time.

It was really a team effort.

I do not know how I ended up here.

They probably made a mistake choosing me.

Here is what I started saying instead:

I earned this seat.

Ownership is not arrogance.

I can be humble and still be clear.

My impact deserves a name, and my name can hold it.

I will not hide behind humility.

Speak the Truth (Reframe): What is the clean, factual sentence I need to say about my impact without shrinking it?

Think. Speak. Manifest.

The truth is: _____

MANIFEST SHIFT: THE OWNERSHIP SCRIPT (COMMIT)

Impostor thoughts lose power when we practice ownership out loud. This is a script to help you prepare before high-visibility moments and respond after them.

Before a Meeting or Presentation

Rehearse your Evidence Inventory silently. Then complete this sentence:

> *"I am in this room because I _____. And my contribution today is _____."*

This is not about ego. It is about grounding. You are reminding yourself why you are there before you walk in.

When Asked What You Do

Resist the urge to minimize. Practice saying one factual, confident sentence about your role or contribution. For example:

"I lead the team that manages our emergency funding distribution."

"I designed the process that serves 16,000 students each year."

"I built the framework our department uses for reporting."

Clean. Factual. No hedging. You are not bragging. You are answering the question.

After Receiving Recognition

When someone acknowledges your work, do not deflect. Practice this response:

"Thank you. I worked hard on that, and I am glad it landed."

This is simple, gracious, and does not give your credit away. You can acknowledge others who helped, but do not make it sound like you had nothing to do with it.

When Impostor Thoughts Get Loud

Try this script with yourself:

"I notice I am feeling like I do not belong. That is fear talking. What is true? I did the work. I have the evidence. I will stand in what I know instead of shrinking from what I feel."

Use this script at least once this week in a real moment. Practice changes posture.

QUICK EXERCISE: THE TWO-COLUMN REFRAME

If you've used the Two-Column Reframe earlier in this book, this is the same tool with a different target. Impostor thinking thrives in private. This puts it on paper so evidence can answer it.

Draw two columns: **The Story I Tell Myself** and **What Is Actually True.**

Write three impostor thoughts you've had recently. Make them specific, not general. Then answer each one with what is true when you're grounded.

Example:

The Story I Tell Myself	What Is Actually True
I only got this role because no one else applied.	I was interviewed, evaluated, and selected. Someone saw my qualifications and made a decision.
If they knew how uncertain I feel, they would not trust me.	Confidence is not the absence of doubt. I have delivered results even while feeling uncertain, and that is the mark of real competence.
I should not take credit because other people helped.	Acknowledging my role does not erase anyone else. Collaboration and ownership can coexist.

Read the right column out loud. Let the evidence land. Circle one truth from the right column and carry it into your next high-visibility moment.

Repeat this whenever impostor thoughts get loud. Over time, the right column becomes your default.

OUTCOME EVIDENCE

When you practice these tools consistently, you should notice:

- More comfort speaking about your contributions in meetings and conversations
- At least one clear statement of impact shared this week, clean and factual

- Reduced shrinking in high-visibility rooms
- Less deflecting when you receive recognition
- A growing sense that you are allowed to take up space

FINAL THOUGHTS

I used to think humility meant staying invisible. I thought that by letting others take credit, I was being gracious. I thought that by shrinking, I was being safe. But shrinking did not protect me. It just kept me from the rooms I had already earned.

The shift for me was not learning to brag. It was learning to tell the truth. Ownership is not arrogance. Ownership is accuracy. And accuracy does not need permission.

You can be humble and still be clear. You can give credit to your team and still acknowledge your role. You can feel uncertain inside and still stand in what you know to be true about what you have done.

You did not slip through. You walked in. And you are allowed to say so.

What Comes Next

You now have tools to challenge perfectionism and impostor thinking. You know how to let good enough move you forward, and you know how to stand in what you've earned. But what happens when the problem is not standards, control, or visibility, and you still can't move? When it's not confusion or fear, but fatigue and burnout? That's where we go next.

SHIFT CHECK

Pause. Reflect. Notice the shift.

Focus: Identity, exposure, and the fear of being found out

THINK (Catch It): Patterns I'm Becoming Aware Of

What part of myself have I been hiding because I am afraid of how people will respond?

_____

_____

Where do I feel like I am performing instead of being real?

_____

_____

SPEAK (Challenge It) Scripts I'm Interrupting

What lie do I keep rehearsing about who I have to be in order to be accepted?

_____

_____

What script plays in my head when I think about being fully seen?

_____

_____

Speak the Truth (Reframe): What is the truth I need to speak back to that script, even if I don't feel it yet?

The truth is:

_____

_____

MANIFEST (Commit): Evidence of Movement

Where did I let someone see the real me this week, without editing myself first?

_____

_____

What mask did I set down, even briefly, and how did it feel?

_____

_____

MANIFEST (Commit): Recommitment

What is one way I will show up more honestly this week?

_____

_____

CHAPTER 10

Catastrophizing Setbacks: When It Feels Like the End

"A setback is not a verdict. It is information."

By now, you know the feeling. One hard moment happens, and before you can even breathe, your mind turns it into a prophecy about how bad things are going to be. If you let your thoughts narrate the story, you'll start sounding like Chicken Little from that old fable: "The sky is falling. The sky is falling." Then life keeps moving, and you realize the sky never fell. This is why the TSM Loop matters. Catch the catastrophe. Challenge the prophecy. Commit to the next right step.

You just got caught in the rehearsal, and psychology has a name for it: catastrophic thinking. It's when the mind overestimates threat, exaggerates consequences, and treats the worst-case story like a forecast. Researchers describe it as a pattern that shows up across many kinds of emotional struggle because it pulls people into prediction instead of presence, and fear starts sounding like fact.[28]

And here's the relief: this chapter will teach you how to pull your thoughts back to what's true, so one setback doesn't hijack your confidence and start steering your future.

But what happens when you make a decision you can't easily own? When the outcome is not applause but disruption? When you did the right thing—and it still hurts?

As you move forward, we will uncover how your mind can turn one painful moment into the belief that everything is ruined.

THE BIG DECISION

There was a time when I was a manager, and I had to make a decision that changed someone's life.

A person needed to be separated from the organization. It was the right decision, but it was still a heavy one. It was not the kind of decision you make and then go home feeling proud. It was emotional. It was disruptive. And truthfully, it was not a decision I wanted to carry.

But I had to.

Once the situation became real, my mind started spiraling.

What are people going to think?
How am I going to navigate this fallout?
What if this blows up everything I am trying to build?

It haunted me. It kept me up at night. I started wanting to retreat from day-to-day engagements because I felt exposed by the decision. Even though the decision was made for good reason, my mind treated it like a disaster.

I did not just think it would impact one person. I started believing it would ruin everything. I began to internalize it like the entire operation was doomed and the culture would never recover.

The emotional weight got to me at my core. I cried behind that decision. I replayed it. I spoke to myself like I had failed. And the hardest part was that the ripple effects were real. There were operational shifts. There was tension. There was disruption. And in my mind, every ripple felt like proof I made the wrong call.

> **Catastrophizing does not prepare you. It drains you.**

For a long time, that decision stayed with me. Years later, it resurfaced enough that I eventually wrote about it in one of my books because I needed to process what it taught me. With time, things stabilized. The culture didn't collapse. The disruption was real, but it wasn't the end. What felt like permanent damage was actually a season of adjustment.

Sometimes leadership requires decisions you do not want to make. Sometimes being responsible does not feel heroic. It feels heavy. And if you do not learn how to reframe setbacks, your mind will convince you that one painful moment means everything is falling apart.

THE MIND TRAP

Catastrophizing is when your mind turns one hard moment into a story that the whole future is ruined. It doesn't just predict the future. It steals your presence.

It takes a setback and makes it a sentence.

You make a difficult decision, and instead of processing the discomfort, your mind projects it forward. It turns a hard day into a hard year. It turns tension into total collapse. It tells you that one disruption means you have lost control of everything.

Worst-case thinking doesn't make you wiser. It paralyzes you with a future that hasn't happened and may never happen. And while you're frozen in that imagined disaster, the real work of stabilizing, communicating, and moving forward is still waiting on you.

WHY THIS HAPPENS

Catastrophizing does not come from weakness. It often comes from responsibility and other contributing factors.

Empathy and emotional responsibility. When you care about the people you lead, their pain becomes your weight. You feel the impact of your decision on their lives, and that feeling can grow until it feels unbearable.

Fear of judgment. *What will people think about me now?* That question can spiral into a thousand imagined conversations, none of which have happened yet. When this occurs, you rehearse their disappointment before they have even spoken.

Leadership pressure. High-stakes decisions come with high-stakes scrutiny. When the outcome is public, the pressure to get it right can turn any misstep into a perceived failure.

Lack of preparedness for fallout. Sometimes you make the right call, but you were not ready for the ripple effects. When the disruption surprises you, your mind fills in the blanks with the worst possible story.

Internalized perfection. If you believe that good leaders prevent all disruption, then any disruption becomes personal failure. That belief is not realistic, but it can feel true when you are in the middle of it.

Rumination. Replaying the moment over and over does not produce new insight. It just makes the moment feel bigger than it is. Each replay reinforces the fear instead of resolving it. And research backs this up. Rumination tends to deepen distress because it fuels negative thinking, weakens problem-solving, and interferes with the behaviors that would actually move you forward. That's why replaying a moment can feel like you're processing, but you're really just rehearsing pain without resolution.[29]

THE COST

Catastrophizing does not just stay in your head. It leaks into your leadership.

Sleeplessness and anxiety become your companions. You lie awake replaying scenarios that have not happened. Your body carries the stress of imagined futures.

You start second-guessing yourself long after the decision is made. Instead of stabilizing the environment, you retreat. Instead of leading through the disruption, you avoid it.

Your confidence as a leader erodes. If you believe that one hard moment has undone everything, you stop trusting your own judgment. That loss of trust makes the next decision even harder.

And the culture disruption you feared? It often feels worse because your mind amplified it. When you expect disaster, you start to see disaster everywhere, even in moments that could have been navigated with steady presence.

The cost is not just how you feel. It is what you fail to do while you are stuck in the spiral.

Think. Speak. Manifest.

THINK SHIFT: THE REFRAME REPORT (CATCH IT)

Here is what helped me when my mind kept telling me everything was falling apart.

The Tool: The Reframe Report

When your mind says, "everything is doomed," write a quick report. One page maximum. Five questions:

1. **Fact:** What actually happened? (Not what you fear. Not what you imagine. What occurred.)
2. **Impact:** What changed because of it? (Be realistic. Name the actual ripple effects.)
3. **Fear Story:** What is my mind predicting? (Write it down. Let the catastrophe have a name.)
4. **Truth:** What is within my control now? (Not what is outside your control. What can you actually influence.)
5. **Next Right Step:** One action to stabilize and move forward.

When to use it: When you catch yourself spiraling after a difficult decision. When you cannot sleep because your mind keeps replaying the worst-case scenario. When the disruption feels bigger than it probably is.

How long it takes: Less than five minutes. Writing forces clarity.

What it produces: Separation between facts and fear. A clearer sense of what you can control. One actionable step instead of a thousand imagined disasters.

Reflection Questions:

1. What is true right now, not what I fear later?
2. Am I confusing discomfort with disaster?

3. If a mentor were watching me, what would they tell me to do next?

SPEAK SHIFT: THE WORDS THAT INTERRUPT THE SPIRAL (CHALLENGE IT)

When my mind is loud, my words matter even more. The language I use with myself can either feed the spiral or interrupt it.

Here are the phrases I stopped saying:

I ruined everything.
People are going to hate me.
This is blowing up the whole operation.
I made the wrong decision.
I cannot recover from this.

Here is what I started saying instead:

This is hard, but it is not the end.
A painful decision can still be the right one.
I can lead through disruption without losing myself.
I am allowed to feel it and still move forward.
I will learn from this and stabilize what needs stabilizing.

Speak the Truth (Reframe): What is the one sentence I need to repeat when my mind says, "This ruined everything"?

The truth is: _____

MANIFEST SHIFT: THE 7-DAY STABILIZATION PLAN (COMMIT)

Catastrophizing loses its grip when you move. This plan is designed to help you regain footing after a difficult decision or setback.

Small Step (Today)

Write the Reframe Report once. One page maximum. Answer all five questions. Let the facts have more space than the fear.

Bold Step (This Week)

Have one grounded conversation to stabilize the environment. This could be with a team member, a peer, or a stakeholder. You goal here is not to defend yourself. It's to set expectations, clarify next steps, and bring calm presence to the disruption.

Before the conversation, complete this sentence: *"What I want them to walk away knowing is _____."*

Consistency Habit (Nightly)

Each night this week, practice "Close the Loop." Before bed, write three things:

- One lesson I learned today.
- One action I took to stabilize.
- One thing I am releasing.

This practice prevents rumination from owning your nights. It gives your mind a place to land instead of running the same loop. There's a reason this works. Studies on bedtime writing show that getting tasks and loose ends out of your head and onto paper can reduce the mental arousal that keeps people awake. In one lab study, people who wrote a specific to-do list for just a few minutes fell asleep faster than those who wrote about completed tasks, which supports what you're doing here: you're giving your brain a safe place to "set it down."[30]

QUICK EXERCISE: THE TRIGGER REPLAY

The Trigger Replay helps you separate the facts of what happened from the fear-filled meaning your mind added afterward. When a hard moment keeps replaying, your brain is usually trying to regain control by rehearsing it. This exercise gives that energy a direction. It helps you name the event, name the story, name the need underneath it, and then choose a next step that puts you back in leadership instead of in self-punishment.

This exercise takes about 10 minutes and helps you process a difficult moment without staying stuck in it.

Step 1: Name the Event

Write one sentence describing what happened. Keep it factual.

Step 2: Name the Story You Told Yourself

Complete: *"The part of this decision that hurt me most was..."*

Complete: *"What I feared people would say was..."*

Step 3: Name What You Needed

Complete: *"What I needed to remember was..."*

Step 4: Name the Next Step

Complete this sentence: *"If I could re-enter that week with wisdom, I would..."*

Example:

Event	I had to separate someone from the organization.
What hurt most	Knowing that my decision affected their life, even if it was the right one.
What I feared	That people would see me as cruel or unfair. That the team would never trust me again.
What I needed	That hard decisions do not make me a bad leader. That disruption is temporary. That I can lead through this.
With wisdom	I would have had a stabilizing conversation sooner. I would have stopped replaying and started leading.

Use this exercise any time a difficult moment keeps replaying in your mind. It moves you from rumination to resolution.

OUTCOME EVIDENCE

After seven days of practicing these tools, you should notice:

- Reduced rumination and replaying of the difficult moment
- Clearer separation between facts and fear
- At least one stabilizing action taken
- A calmer sense of leadership presence
- Better sleep and less anxiety about imagined futures

CONCLUDING THOUGHTS

I used to believe that feeling the weight of a decision meant I had made the wrong one. I thought good leaders moved through hard moments without emotion, without doubt, without nights spent replaying the scene. That was not true. Good leaders feel the weight. They just do not let the weight become the whole story.

A setback is not a verdict. It is information. And information can be processed, learned from, and used to stabilize what comes next. The hard moment does not have to define your leadership. How you move through it does.

I prayed, and then I moved. I wrote the report. I had the conversation. I closed the loop each night until the spiral loosened and I could breathe again. You can do the same. You can feel the weight and still move forward. You can lead through disruption without losing yourself. That is the work.

Catch it. Challenge it. Commit.

Time to Look Closer

You now have tools for when setbacks feel like the end. You know how to separate facts from fear and how to stabilize after a hard decision. But what happens when the challenge is not a single moment? Or when the issue is not clarity or fear but depletion and burnout? That is what we expose next.

CHAPTER 11

When It's All or Nothing

"Consistency is quieter than hype, but it wins."

You ever notice how one setback can make you question your whole ability? One slow week, one rough result, and you start thinking, Maybe this isn't for me. That's all-or-nothing thinking. It convinces you that if it's not going well right now, it's never going to go well at all. In a study, researchers found that people writing in online spaces about anxiety, depression, and suicidal ideation spaces used more absolutist words (think always, never, completely, nothing) than control groups. The point is not that words cause the struggle.[31] It's that all-or-nothing thinking shows up in how we talk, and it becomes a reliable fingerprint of a mind that is trying to make uncertainty feel final.

That's why the TSM Loop matters here. Catch the absolutist thought. Challenge the verdict. Commit to the next week of consistency.

And you see it everywhere. In sports, in business, in relationships, in personal growth. The moment it doesn't feel like a win, your emotions want an immediate conclusion, so you start backing out of things that would have worked if you stayed steady.

This chapter is about staying in the game long enough for consistency to do its job.

THE BUSINESS ENDEAVOR

I've got a friend named Jacob who wanted to turn travel into a side business. He was a buddy who took trips with me, and along the way he started learning how people were building income by helping others book their vacations. It made sense to him. He already worked a full-time job, but he wanted something he could grow over time, something that could bring in extra income without him having to clock in for every dollar.

So he did what a lot of motivated people do when they finally see a door crack open. He invested. He bought courses, learned the process, built his pages, and started telling people, "Book your trips with me." In the beginning, it actually worked. A couple people booked, and when that commission hit, it felt like confirmation. Like, okay, I'm onto something. This might really be it.

That's when Jacob doubled down. He stayed up later than usual, studied more, posted more, reached out more, and tried to sharpen everything. He wasn't afraid of hard work, and he knew businesses take time. But after a while, the bookings slowed down. People stopped responding. Some went back to booking the way they always had. And that's when his mind started treating the slowdown like a message.

Nobody wants to book with me.
I wasted my money on these courses.
If this was really for me, it would be moving faster.

And because it wasn't moving at the pace he expected, he began questioning the whole journey.

He didn't stop because he didn't have potential. He stopped because the silence felt personal. Putting in effort without seeing results started to feel like proof that it wasn't working at all. Even thinking about starting again felt heavy because the same fear showed up every time.

What if I put in all that work and it still doesn't move? he said.

That's all-or-nothing thinking. If it's not a clear win, it feels like a waste. If it's not going up, it must be failing. And that mindset will shut down momentum even when growth is still underway. And if I'm being honest, I've had my own version of that too. Jacob didn't fail. He hit a normal dip and treated it like a verdict. That's what this mindset does. It turns a pause into a conclusion.

THE MIND TRAP

All-or-nothing thinking does not come from laziness. It often comes from caring too much about the wrong measurement: speed.

It turns normal fluctuations into reasons to quit. The thought isn't just loud. It's final. And final thinking kills momentum.

When you are in this pattern, a slow week feels like a failed vision. A dip in engagement feels like proof that you were wrong to try. One disappointing result becomes enough evidence to abandon something that was still building.

This kind of thinking does not protect you from failure. It creates it. This is also where mindset matters. Research on "implicit theories" explains that when people believe ability or success is fixed, setbacks can trigger a helpless pattern that sounds like, "Maybe this isn't for me." But when people hold a growth-oriented view, setbacks are more likely to be interpreted as feedback, not identity. That shift does not erase disappointment, but it keeps disappointment from becoming a conclusion.[32] Because the truth is, most things that grow do not grow in a straight line. They build, they dip, they adjust, and they rise again. But if your mind only accepts upward, you will walk away from projects, ideas, and visions that had more life in them than you allowed.

WHY THIS HAPPENS

All-or-nothing thinking does not come from laziness. It often comes from caring too much about the wrong measurement, chasing results for validation. When your confidence depends on views, likes, and growth, every dip becomes personal. You stop measuring mission and start measuring metrics. And metrics fluctuate. They always do. So if your mind only feels safe when the numbers are up, you will keep treating normal dips like proof you should stop.

Attaching meaning to metrics instead of mission. When numbers become the scoreboard for your worth, a slow period can feel like a verdict on your value. You forget that impact is not always visible in real time.

Fear of looking unsuccessful. If people are watching, you might feel pressure to either win publicly or disappear quietly. Staying consistent through a slow season feels vulnerable. Quitting feels cleaner.

Impatience with slow-building outcomes. We live in a world that celebrates overnight success and viral moments. That makes steady progress feel invisible. If growth is not fast, it can feel like failure, even when it is real.

Exhaustion and limited bandwidth. When you are tired, quitting can feel like relief. All-or-nothing thinking gives your exhaustion a reason: *See? It was not working anyway.* That makes walking away feel justified instead of premature.

Perfectionism overlap. This connects to what we covered earlier: if it is not "winning," it feels like "failing." But that binary leaves no room for building, adjusting, or learning. And those are exactly the stages where most real progress happens.

THE COST

All-or-nothing thinking does not protect your time or energy. It wastes both.

You abandon projects that could have matured. Some ideas need time to build momentum. Some audiences need time to find you. When you walk away at the first dip, you never find out what could have grown if you had kept going.

You lose consistency and audience-building momentum. Every restart costs you. The people who were beginning to pay attention move on. The algorithm that was beginning to learn your content resets. You trade compound progress for repeated fresh starts.

You increase self-doubt about future ideas. Every quit leaves a mark. The next time you have a creative spark, part of your mind will whisper, *Remember last time? You quit that one too*. And that voice makes it harder to begin again.

You tie your worth to outcomes, which leads to emotional burnout. When every dip feels like personal failure, creating becomes exhausting. You stop enjoying the work because the work is no longer about the mission. It is about the scoreboard.

THINK SHIFT: THE TREND VS. MISSION FILTE (CATCH IT)

Here is what helped me when my mind wanted to treat every dip like a death sentence.

The Tool: The Trend vs. Mission Filter

When you feel the urge to quit, pause and ask yourself one question: *Am I doing this for metrics, or for impact?*

Then work through these three filters:

- **If nobody praised it this week, would I still believe it matters?**
  This separates validation from vision. If the answer is yes, the mission is still worth pursuing.
- **What result am I chasing, and what result can I control?**
  You cannot control views or engagement. You can control consistency, quality, and showing up. Shift your focus to what is in your hands.
- **What does "working" actually mean in the first 90 days?**
  Most things take time to build. Define realistic success for the season you are in, not the season you wish you were in.

When to use it: When you feel the urge to quit something that has not been given a fair runway. When results dip and your mind says, *This is not working.* When you are measuring success by hype instead of progress.

How long it takes: Less than five minutes. Ask the three questions. Write the answers if needed.

What it produces: Clarity about whether you are quitting because the mission is wrong or because the metrics are not cooperating. A decision rooted in purpose, not frustration.

Reflection Questions:
1. What did I expect too fast?
2. What would steady progress look like without hype?
3. What if the dip is normal, not a sign to stop?

SPEAK SHIFT : WHAT YOU SAY DURING THE DIP (CHALLENGE IT)

When my mind is loud, my words matter even more. The language I use with myself can either reinforce the all-or-nothing pattern or interrupt it.

And there's research behind this kind of talk and thinking. Studies on self-compassion show that responding to failure with an honest, kind, steady stance can actually increase motivation to improve. It's a quiet paradox. When you stop beating yourself up for the dip, you get more willing to stay with the work. That's why these statements matter. They aren't hype. They're a healthier inner climate for consistency to grow in.[33]

Below, I show how we tend to frame this through negative self-talk, then how to reframe it in a healthier way.

What I stopped saying:

This is a waste of time.

Nobody cares.

If it's not popping, it's pointless.

I'm not cut out for this.

I should stop.

What I started saying instead:

One slow week is not a failed vision.

I am building a body of work, not chasing one moment.
Consistency creates trust.
I can adjust without quitting.
My purpose does not rise and fall with views.

Speak the Truth (Reframe): What is the truest sentence I can say about this dip without turning it into a verdict?

The truth is: _____

MANIFEST SHIFT: THE WEEKLY EXPERIMENT (COMMIT)

All-or-nothing thinking loses its power when you replace "quit or win" with "test and learn." This weekly experiment helps you stay in motion without needing immediate results.

The Practice: 7 Days Without Checking the Scoreboard

Choose one creative or visibility project you have been tempted to quit. For one week, commit to the following:

1. **Produce at your chosen pace.**
   This could be one post a day, three posts this week, or one video. Pick what is sustainable. If seven days feels intense, start with 48 hours. Two days of not checking the scoreboard still breaks the addiction—and proves you can keep moving without constant feedback.
2. **Do not check metrics for 7 days.**
   No views. No likes. No comments. Let the work exist without immediate judgment.
3. **At the end of the week, review and refine.**
   Instead of "quit or keep going," ask: What did I learn? What can I adjust? What felt sustainable?

The Scorecard (fill in at end of week):

Question	Your Answer
How many pieces of content did I create this week?	
Did I resist checking metrics for the full 7 days? (Yes/Partial/No)	
What did I learn about my consistency this week?	
What is one adjustment I want to make next week?	
Am I continuing, adjusting, or pausing? (Circle one)	

Notice that "quitting" is not on the scorecard. The options are continue, adjust, or pause. This reframes the decision away from all-or-nothing.

QUICK EXERCISE: THE MIND DUMP AND SORT

If you've done the Mind Dump + Sort earlier, this is the same reset with a different purpose. When all-or-nothing thinking shows up, emotions start sounding like facts. This exercise separates volume from truth so you can make one wise adjustment instead of quitting.

Set a timer for three minutes. Write everything your mind is saying about the project, idea, or goal you feel tempted to abandon. Do not filter. Do not edit. Just dump it onto the page.

Example: "This is pointless. Nobody watches. I'm embarrassed. I should have never started. Other people do this better. It's a waste of my time. I look stupid."

Now organize your responses into three columns labeled Noise, Truth, and Next Step. Noise is the emotional reaction. Truth is the legitimate feedback worth considering. Next Step is your actionable plan for moving forward.

When completed, your table should resemble the example below.

Example:

Noise (emotional, reaction, not fact)	Truth (legitimate feedback or data)	Next Step (actionable adjustment)
"I look stupid."	Views dropped after the first few posts.	Test a different posting time or format.
"This is pointless."	I have not given it 90 days yet.	Commit to 30 more days before deciding.

Then act only on the **Next Step** column. That is your forward motion. Use this any time your mind floods with reasons to quit. It helps you see what is real and what is just volume.

OUTCOME EVIDENCE

After one week of practicing these tools, you should notice:

- At least one restarted action (a post, video, script, or piece of content) completed
- Reduced dependence on metrics for confidence
- Increased consistency for one full week
- A clearer definition of success beyond hype
- A shift from "quit or win" thinking to "test and learn" thinking

FINAL WRAP-UP

I still think about a project I started—my 'Leadership Baby.' I still believe the concept could work. And I still wrestle with whether to pick it back up or let it rest.

What I do not wrestle with anymore is the belief that one dip means total failure.

That is the shift. I can look at something that did not go the way I hoped and still see value in it. I can acknowledge that the metrics dropped and still believe in the mission. I can decide to pause without telling myself I wasted my time.

Consistency is quieter than hype, but it wins. And the people who build things that last are the ones who stay in motion while everyone else walks away at the first slow week.

You can adjust without quitting. You can rest without abandoning. And you can define success on your own terms, not by the scoreboard.

What Comes Next

You now have tools for all-or-nothing thinking. You know how to separate mission from metrics and how to stay in motion when results dip. But what happens when the voice telling you to quit is not about outcomes? What happens when the voice is about

Think. Speak. Manifest.

you? When the loudest critic is not external but internal? When the pattern is not about performance but about how you speak to yourself? Let's take time to unpack that next.

CHAPTER 12

The Not-Enough Script

"Sometimes the risk isn't the opportunity. Sometimes the risk is believing you're worth it."

You write the email. You read it twice. You fix one sentence. You add a comma. You reread it again. Then your finger hovers over "Send," and something in you says, Maybe later. You tell yourself you're being careful. You tell yourself you're being professional. But deep down, it's not the email you're editing. It's your willingness to be seen.

If you've ever done that, you've already met the "not enough" script. That's the TSM Loop. Catch the "not enough" script. Challenge the protection voice. Commit to one small step anyway.

And the tricky part is you don't hear it as an insult. You hear it as realism. Maybe I should wait. Maybe I need more time. Maybe I'm not there yet. It sounds responsible, even mature, until you realize how often that same voice shows up right before growth.

Over time, the "not enough" script becomes your inner narrator. It explains why you should shrink, why you should hesitate, why you should stay safe instead of stretching. But here's what most people miss: that voice isn't trying to destroy you. It's trying to protect you, protecting you from being seen, from failing, from trying and discovering it didn't go the way you hoped.

The problem is, protection without permission turns into a prison. If you don't learn to recognize the "not enough" script for what it is, it will quietly make your decisions for you long before you realize you've stopped choosing.

This chapter isn't about silencing that voice. It's about learning not to let it drive.

THE SELF-LOVE EXPERIMENT

For years, I did not fully believe in myself.

That is hard to say out loud, but it is true. Investing in myself felt risky. I had dreams. A part of me just questioned whether I was worth the investment.

I would go back and forth internally. Some days I felt strong. Other days I felt like I was not enough. And when you feel like you are not enough, you do not naturally want to pour into yourself. You start treating your own growth like it is optional.

I bought a rug that says, "Self-Love Club." It is shaped like a black heart with white writing. I put it in my room because I needed a reminder of who I am, what I carry, and who God says I am when my mind tries to tell me something else.

When I look back, I can see roots.

Not having consistent reassurance growing up. Not having people regularly say, "I love you," "You're amazing," "You have potential." Even now, as an adult, I can feel how much I still crave reassurance sometimes. A simple "you did a good job" can hit deeper than people realize.

So investing in myself felt like a gamble. Like I was the risk.

But something started shifting when I began thinking about professional growth and the next level of my career. I decided to bet on myself. I applied for a fellowship, and I got accepted. Research uncovered what I did in that moment. It's called self-efficacy, the belief that you can take the steps required to succeed.[34] A major meta-analysis found that stronger self-efficacy reliably connects to stronger performance, in part because people persist longer when the work gets uncomfortable.

And what hit me was this: I almost avoided that step for years. I wanted it. I just didn't trust myself enough to believe I deserved it or could carry it.

That is what scarcity does in the mind. It tells you, *"Don't spend on you. Don't risk it. Don't step forward."* And it keeps you living beneath what you were built for.

THE MIND TRAP

Scarcity mindset is the belief that resources, opportunities, confidence, or worth are limited, and you may not have enough to invest in yourself. Did you know behavioral science backs this up? Research suggests that scarcity doesn't only change what you have, it changes what you can see.[35] It also shows that when people feel like they have too little, their attention 'tunnels' toward immediate concerns, and that tunnel vision makes bigger, long-term decisions feel riskier than they actually are.[36]

It makes you hesitant to step forward because you treat yourself like a risk. And when you treat yourself like a risk, you start postponing your own future.

When you are in this pattern, self-investment feels dangerous. Spending money on a course, applying for a fellowship, hiring a coach, buying the equipment you need, or even giving yourself time to grow feels like a gamble you might lose. So you wait. You delay. You tell yourself you will do it when you feel more confident, more ready, or more certain.

But that certainty never comes. Because scarcity is not about the resource. It is about the story you believe about yourself. And that story keeps you small while you wait for permission that was already yours.

WHY THIS HAPPENS

Scarcity thinking does not come from weakness. It often comes from history.

Lack of reassurance earlier in life. If you did not hear "I believe in you" or "You have what it takes" consistently, something in you may have learned that investment in you is uncertain. That absence can create a quiet doubt that follows you into adulthood.

Internalized "not enough" narratives. Over time, the absence of external affirmation can become an internal belief. You stop waiting for others to say you are not enough. You say it to yourself before they get the chance.

Fear of wasting money or time on yourself. If you have ever struggled financially or felt like resources were limited, the idea of spending on your own development can feel reckless. You might give freely to others but hesitate to invest in yourself.

Fear of disappointment if you try and fall short. If you do not invest, you cannot fail. Scarcity thinking can be a way to stay safe: stay low, expect less, and avoid the pain of falling short.

Learned survival habits. Some of us learned to only invest in what feels guaranteed. We save our resources for certainties. But personal growth is never guaranteed. It requires risk. And if you only invest in guarantees, you will never invest in yourself.

Craving external validation to confirm internal worth. When you do not fully believe in yourself, you look for others to confirm that you are worth it. But that confirmation is inconsistent. And waiting for it keeps you stuck.

THE COST

Scarcity thinking does not protect you from loss. It guarantees it. You delay growth and miss opportunities. The fellowship I almost avoided? It changed my trajectory. But I almost let years pass before I applied because I did not believe I was worth the risk. How many opportunities have you let pass while waiting to feel ready?

You hold back from investing in skills, exposure, and development. While others are learning, building, and expanding, you stay where you are. It isn't that you lack ability. You've just struggled to believe that your growth matters.

You live with inconsistent confidence and self-trust. Some days you feel strong. Other days you feel like you are not enough. That inconsistency makes it hard to sustain momentum. You keep starting and stopping because your belief in yourself keeps fluctuating.

You stay safe instead of expanding. And safety becomes a ceiling. You were not built to live beneath what is possible for you. But scarcity thinking will keep you there unless you interrupt it.

When the "not enough" script shows up today, don't argue with it—name it, and take one small step anyway.

THINK SHIFT: THE WORTHINESS AUDIT (CATCH IT)

Here is what helped me when my mind kept telling me I was not worth the investment.

The Tool: The Worthiness Audit

When scarcity thinking tries to stop you from investing in yourself, take five minutes to write two lists side by side.

List 1: Evidence I Am Worth Investing In

Write down facts. Not feelings. Not hopes. Facts. What have you accomplished? What have you survived? What impact have you made? What skills do you carry? What have others trusted you with?

Example:

- I have led teams through difficult seasons.
- I have completed degrees while working full time.
- People have asked me for advice because they trust my perspective.
- I have shown up for others even when it was hard.

List 2: Old Stories I Am Still Living Under

Write down the narratives that hold you back. Name them. Where did they come from? Are they still true?

Example:

> *I'm not smart enough to compete at that level.* (from early school experiences)

People like me don't get those opportunities. (from limited representation)

I should wait until I'm ready. (from fear of failure)

When to use it: Before making a decision about investing in yourself. When you feel the pull to say, "not yet" or "not me." When scarcity thinking is louder than your purpose.

How long it takes: Five minutes. Write both lists. Read them out loud.

What it produces: Clarity about whether your hesitation is based on evidence or old stories. A stronger case for betting on yourself.

Reflection Questions:

1. What version of me am I protecting by staying small?
2. What would I do if I believed I was worth it?
3. Who benefits if I finally invest in myself?

SPEAK SHIFT: THE WORDS THAT BUILD SELF-TRUST (CHALLENGE IT)

The language I use with myself either feeds the scarcity story or starves it. I had to learn to stop rehearsing doubt and start rehearsing truth.

Here are the phrases I stopped saying:

I'm not worth the investment.
What if I waste money and still fail?
Other people are more deserving.
I'll wait until I'm more confident.
I don't want to be disappointed.

Here is what I started saying instead:

I am worth investing in.

Confidence grows when I keep my commitments to myself.

I can be scared and still bet on me.

God did not put purpose in me for it to sit.

I am building forward, not waiting for permission.

Speak the Truth (Reframe): What is the one sentence I need to say when my mind whispers, "Not you"?

The truth is: _____

MANIFEST SHIFT: THE 24-HOUR RESET (COMMIT)

Scarcity thinking loses its grip when you act. This reset helps you move within 24 hours, before the old stories can talk you out of it.

Step 1: The Free Investment (This Morning)

Spend 30 minutes on one investment that costs nothing but your attention. Choose one:

- Update your resume or LinkedIn profile
- Outline one speaking topic or content idea
- Review your portfolio or past work
- Practice a skill you have been meaning to sharpen
- Research one opportunity you have been curious about

Thirty minutes. No money required. Just you deciding you matter enough to show up.

Step 2: The Real Investment (Today)

Before the day ends, make one real investment. This is the bet-on-yourself move. Choose one:

- Apply for one opportunity (fellowship, job, program, grant)
- Enroll in one course or training
- Submit one pitch, proposal, or piece of work
- Register for one event, conference, or networking opportunity
- Schedule one conversation that could open a door

One move. Before the day ends. Let your action speak louder than your doubt.

Step 3: The Daily Self-Deposit (Starting Tonight)

Before bed tonight, write one sentence answering this question: *"What is one small thing I did today that showed I am worth my own effort?"*

Do this for a week. Let the evidence accumulate.

QUICK EXERCISE: LETTER TO YOUNGER ME

This exercise takes about 10 minutes and helps you speak to the part of you that first learned you were not enough. This is not about rewriting history. It's about rewriting what you carried forward from it. And this isn't just a sentimental moment. Studies on self-compassionate letter-writing show that practicing this kind of writing can reduce shame and self-criticism and can ease anxiety over time. That's why this matters. A gentler inner voice doesn't just feel better, it makes movement possible.[37]

Step 1: Choose an Age

Think of a younger version of yourself who needed to hear that they were worth it. Maybe it was 10-year-old you. Maybe it was 16-year-old you. Maybe it was the version of you who first felt like they were not enough.

Step 2: Write a Short Letter

Write 5 to 7 sentences directly to that younger version of yourself. Tell them what you wish they had heard. Tell them what you know now that they did not know then. Tell them what is coming.

Example:

> "Hey, younger me. I know you don't hear 'I'm proud of you' as often as you need to. I know you wonder if you're enough. I want you to know that you are. The things you're dreaming about they're going to happen. Everything won't go perfectly. You're still going to get there because you keep showing up. You'll learn how to bet on yourself, even when it's scary. One day, you're going to look back and realize you were always worth it. I love you. Keep going."

Step 3: Read It Out Loud

Read the letter to yourself out loud. Let it land. You do not have to wait for someone else to say it. You can say it now.

OUTCOME EVIDENCE

After practicing these tools, you should notice:

- At least one self-investment action completed
- Improved self-talk around worth and deserving
- Reduced hesitation about growth opportunities
- One "bet on me" move made
- Less hesitation the next time an opportunity asks you to bet on yourself

MY REFLECTIONS

I still have that rug in my room. The black heart with white writing. "Self-Love Club." I step on it every day. I haven't arrived. I just need the reminder sometimes. Some mornings I feel it. Other mornings I have to choose it. Either way, I'm no longer waiting for someone else to tell me I'm worth the investment.

I am telling myself.

The fellowship I almost avoided changed my trajectory. The bet I almost did not make opened doors I could not see at the time. And I would have missed all of it if I had stayed in the scarcity story.

You are worth investing in.

You don't have to be perfect, and you don't have to have it all figured out. God didn't put purpose in you for it to sit. And the only way to find out what's possible is to stop treating yourself like a risk and start treating yourself like someone worth betting on.

You can be scared and still bet on yourself. That is how confidence is built. One self-deposit at a time.

A Step Further

You now have tools for scarcity thinking. You know how to interrupt the "not enough" story and take action before doubt can stop you. But what happens when the pattern is not about investing in yourself? What happens when the pattern is about how you respond to others?

Next, let's unpack together what to do when you keep saying yes when you really mean no. When you absorb everyone else's

Think. Speak. Manifest.

needs and lose yourself in the process. These are the moments that teach us how to win the battle in our mind.

Catch it. Challenge it. Commit.

SHIFT CHECK

Pause. Reflect. Notice the shift.

Focus: Perfectionism, "not enough," and internal pressure

THINK (Catch It): Patterns I'm Becoming Aware Of

Where am I holding myself to a standard that no one else is asking me to meet?

_____

_____

What have I been delaying because it does not feel ready or good enough yet?

_____

_____

SPEAK (Challenge It): Scripts I'm Interrupting

What do I keep telling myself about what I need to fix before I can move?

_____

_____

What phrase do I repeat that keeps raising the bar instead of letting me begin?

_____

_____

Speak the Truth (Reframe): What is the truth I need to speak back to that script, even if I don't feel it yet?

The truth is:

_____

_____

MANIFEST (Commit): Evidence of Movement

Evidence of Movement Where did I choose progress over perfection this week?

_____

_____

What did I release, finish, or share even though it was not flawless?

_____

_____

MANIFEST (Commit): Recommitment

What is one thing I will stop over-preparing and simply do?

_____

_____

CHAPTER 13

When Comfort Betrays Your Growth

"The old me kept me safe. The next me is supposed to take me forward."

It's time to tell the truth. And sometimes the truth hurts, because it forces you to face who you've been, what it has cost you, and what you're ready to become. Even when you finally bet on yourself, your mind can still pull you backward.

Growth gets hard when the next version of you requires a goodbye, not only to habits, but to identities and roles you've worn for so long they started to feel like you. And the truth is, sometimes you're not clinging to what is unhealthy because you love it. You're clinging to it because it once protected you. Research supports this. Identity-based motivation theory shows that when a new action feels identity-congruent, difficulty feels meaningful. But when it feels identity-incongruent, the same difficulty can sound like, 'This isn't for people like me,' which is exactly how comfort convinces you to stay put.[38] This is where the TSM Loop becomes a mirror. Catch the loyalty. Challenge the comfort script. Commit to becoming.

You can build the thing, launch the vision, take the step forward—and still find yourself retreating. Not always because you doubt your worth. Sometimes it's because a part of you is still loyal to an older version of yourself that no longer fits your future.

So let's name the trap. Why do we stay committed to who we were when it keeps costing us who we are becoming?

THE FORTUNE TELLER MOMENT

I have always known something about myself. When I get into a routine, I can be good at what I do. I get comfortable in how I live, how I move, how I speak. That comfort has protected me. It has given me stability. It has helped me build a strong professional reputation. It has helped me serve students in higher education. And it gave me a lane I knew how to drive in. This is also how habits work. Research shows that repeated behaviors become tied to the *context* you do them in, so the environment starts cueing the same response automatically. That's why the lane you've driven in for years can feel like peace, even when it's really just a well-rehearsed pattern.[39]

But that old version of me came with a limit.

Because the familiar does not just protect you. It can also become a wall. It can keep you from exploring other realms, expanding your thinking, reaching for what you said you wanted, and becoming who you know you are. Behavioral research calls this *status quo bias,* which is our tendency to stick with the current option because change feels riskier than staying put, even when staying put is costing us. That's how the familiar can protect you and imprison you at the same time.[40]

I saw that clearly a couple of years ago.

I was in New Orleans with friends, walking near Bourbon Street. I saw a convenience store, and in the back there was a psychic offering readings. I went in for kicks and giggles. The lesson is about movement, not mystique.

WHEN COMFORT BETRAYS YOUR GROWTH

I told my friends I was going to do it, just to see what would happen.

I sat down, and the psychic asked me what I did.

Then she said something that caught me off guard. She said she saw me on a stage, speaking to large crowds, influencing them, making a difference. She described me in a space that felt bigger than my current comfort zone. And it hit hard because at that very moment in my real life, I was already thinking about *DrKeySpeaks*, my public speaking platform, and had already met with my website designer to start the process.

When I told her what I was already doing, it hit me that I didn't need a stranger to see it. I needed me to stop doubting it.

I left that moment shocked. It felt like life came full circle. But then the real battle started. Not outside of me. Inside of me.

When it came time to actually move forward, my mind pushed back.

You're not ready.
Nobody's going to believe in you.
Who do you think you are?
Stay where you're safe.

So even though I built the website, even though I had the vision, I retreated. I paused. I walked away. I let it sit dormant. Eventually it shut down, and I did not pick it back up because I believed I could not move forward.

That is loyalty to the old version.

The part of me that was comfortable in higher education. The part of me that knew how to stay reliable, professional, consistent, and safe. That version protected me, but it could not open the doors I was supposed to walk through next.

A couple years later, I had to face the truth.

My brand, *DrKeySpeaks*, was never a hobby. It's part of who I am. It's connected to purpose. And I knew that if I kept choosing safety, I would keep delaying what I was born to do.

So I restarted it. I relaunched the platform, started posting again, and took the first speaking step I had been avoiding. The fear was still there. I had just reached the point where I understood the old me couldn't lead me into the future.

THE MIND TRAP

Loyalty to the old version is when you stay committed to what feels safe, even when it no longer fits who you are becoming.

It feels like stability, but it can become stagnation. Stagnation is what comfort looks like when it stops serving your calling.

Here is what makes this one hard to see: the old version actually worked. It served you. It kept you employed, respected, grounded. It gave you a track record. The problem is when that version becomes a ceiling instead of a foundation. When you keep honoring who you were at the expense of who you are supposed to become.

Letting go of something that worked feels like betrayal. But sometimes it is the most obedient thing you can do. Obedience is not always dramatic. Sometimes it is simply choosing growth over comfort.

WHY THIS HAPPENS

Loyalty to the old version does not come from laziness. It often comes from success.

WHEN COMFORT BETRAYS YOUR GROWTH

Comfort becomes identity. When you have been doing something well for a long time, it starts to feel like who you are. "I am the higher education professional." "I am the reliable one." "I am the person who stays in their lane." That identity kept you employed and respected. But it cannot take you where purpose is calling you next.

Fear of visibility and new arenas. Stepping into something new means being seen in a new way. And being seen comes with risk. What if people judge you? What if you fail publicly? The old version kept you safe from that exposure.

Unfamiliar success feels risky. You know how to succeed in your current lane. You have the receipts. But the next version requires skills, relationships, and visibility you have not tested yet. That uncertainty can feel more dangerous than staying where you are.

Internal doubts about readiness and credibility. *Who do you think you are?* That question can stop you before you start. The old version does not ask that question because the old version already has answers. The new version has to earn them.

> **Comfort becomes dangerous when it starts to feel like peace.**

Staying safe is rewarded. Society often rewards consistency over growth. You get praised for reliability, not for risk. So stepping out can feel like rebellion, even when it is alignment with who you are meant to be.

Purpose requires expansion, and expansion requires discomfort. Who you are becoming cannot be reached from within the old comfort zone. Something has to stretch. And stretching does not feel safe.

THE COST

Loyalty to the old version does not protect your future. It delays it. Dormant dreams stay dormant. The vision you carry does not disappear just because you do not act on it. It waits. And while it waits, time passes. Opportunities close. And the regret builds quietly in the background.

You miss opportunities to build impact. The people you were supposed to reach, the stages you were supposed to stand on, the work you were supposed to create, all of that waits while you stay loyal to a version of yourself that was never meant to be permanent.

You carry regret from ignoring the inner pull. There is a cost to knowing you were meant for more and choosing comfort anyway. That cost does not show up on a bill. It shows up in quiet moments when you wonder what would have happened if you had just moved.

You stay confined to one lane when you were built for more. The old version gave you a lane. But purpose often requires multiple lanes, new roads, and territories you have never driven before. If you stay where you are, you will never find out what else was possible.

THINK SHIFT: THE OLD ME INVENTORY (CATCH IT)

Here is what helped me when the familiar kept pulling me backward.

WHEN COMFORT BETRAYS YOUR GROWTH

The Tool: The Old Me Inventory

I want you to do this when you feel stuck between who you were and who you are becoming, because it will help you change your behavior. The science behind this exercise is called decisional balance, and studies show that as people move toward real change, the perceived pros of change rise while the cons lose their grip. In other words, this tool helps your mind stop romanticizing comfort and start telling the truth about cost.[41] Now take five minutes to write the two lists below.

List 1: What the Old Version Protected Me From

Be honest. The old version was not useless. It served a purpose. What did it shield you from? What risks did it help you avoid? What stability did it provide?

Example:

- Public failure
- Being judged for stepping outside my lane
- Financial uncertainty
- The discomfort of being a beginner again

List 2: What the Old Version Is Now Costing Me

Be equally honest here. The old version had benefits, but it also has a price. What is staying the same costing you now?

Example:

- Delayed purpose
- A platform that sat dormant for years
- Regret from knowing I could do more
- Impact I never made because I stayed safe

When to use it: When you feel pulled toward something new, but your mind keeps retreating to what is familiar. When you catch yourself saying "I am not ready" for something you have wanted for years.

How long it takes: Five minutes. Write both lists. Compare them.

What it produces: Clarity about whether you are being protected or held back. A clearer case for moving forward.

Reflection Questions:
1. What part of me is trying to stay safe right now?
2. What does who I am becoming need that who I was cannot provide?
3. If I keep choosing comfort for another year, what will I lose?

SPEAK SHIFT: WHAT I SAY WHEN COMFORT CALLS ME BACK (CHALLENGE IT)

The words I speak to myself either anchor me to who I was or release me into who I am becoming. I had to learn to stop rehearsing safety and start rehearsing movement.

Here are the phrases I stopped saying:

I'm not ready yet.

Nobody will believe in me.

I should stay in my lane.

I'll do it later.

This is too much.

Here is what I started saying instead:

Comfort served me, but I am called to grow.

I can be new and still be gifted.

Purpose does not require perfection. It requires obedience and movement.

I do not need full confidence to take one step.

I am becoming. I am not shrinking.

Speak the Truth (Reframe): What is the sentence I need to say when my old version tries to negotiate me back into safety?

The truth is: _____

MANIFEST SHIFT: THE 7-DAY BECOMING PLAN (COMMIT)

Loyalty to the old version loses its grip when you start living as who you are becoming. This plan helps you take tangible steps toward that.

Small Step (Today)

Write one paragraph defining your "next version." Answer these questions in your paragraph:

- What does the next version of me do that the current version avoids?
- What does the next version create, build, or share weekly?
- How does the next version show up when fear says retreat?

Keep this paragraph somewhere visible. It is your compass.

Bold Step (This Week)

Restart one dormant platform or project with one concrete action. Choose one:

- Post one piece of content
- Send one email about your vision
- Create or reactivate one booking link or landing page
- Record one video, even if you do not publish it yet
- Reach out to one person about collaboration or opportunity

One action this week. It does not have to be perfect. It just has to be movement.

Do the action in private first. Draft the post but don't publish it yet. Record the video but keep it in your camera roll. Write the email and save it as a draft. The primary focus is still movement—just with less exposure while you build strength.

Consistency Habit (Weekly)

Block 60 minutes each week for a "Becoming Block." During this hour, do one action that only who you are becoming would do. Something who you were would avoid. Something that stretches you toward the future.

Put it on your calendar and guard it. That hour is where the old version starts losing its grip.

QUICK EXERCISE: THE TWO-COLUMN REFRAME

When you feel pulled back toward what's familiar, this exercise helps you put that inner debate on paper. It separates the voice of who you were from the truth of who you are becoming so you can move forward with clarity.

Draw two columns.

On the left write: **What the Old Version Says.**

On the right write: **What the Next Version Knows.**

Write 3 to 5 statements in each column. Be specific. Let the contrast be clear.

Example:

What the Old Version Says	What the Next Version Knows
"You're not ready."	Readiness grows through action, not waiting.
"Stay in your lane."	I can expand my lane without losing my foundation.
"Nobody will believe in you."	I do not need everyone to believe. I need to believe and move.
"It's too late."	The only deadline on purpose is the one I set by not moving.

Read the right column out loud. Let the truth land. The old version has been speaking for a long time. Now who you are becoming gets to respond.

OUTCOME EVIDENCE

After practicing these tools, you should notice:

- One revived action taken toward purpose
- Reduced hesitation around stepping into visibility
- Clearer self-definition beyond comfort
- A written description of who you are becoming that you can return to

- A weekly rhythm that moves you forward

AFTER THE READING

I walked into that psychic reading for fun and walked out carrying a confirmation I wasn't sure I was ready to hold. I'm not sharing this because the source is the point. I'm sharing it because the moment exposed something true: I could say what I wanted all day, but I still had to move.

Then I did what many of us do. I built the thing, felt the fear, and retreated to what felt safe. DrKeySpeaks sat dormant for years, not because the vision was wrong, but because I was still loyal to a version of myself that couldn't carry it.

When I restarted, I didn't have all the answers. But I finally understood this: who I was couldn't take me where I was called to go. The safety that once protected me had become the wall blocking what I was built for.

You don't have to abandon who you were, but you do have to loosen the grip it has on who you're becoming. The next version of you isn't far. It's one honest step away.

What's Next

You have tools now for releasing loyalty to old versions of yourself. But what happens when the obstacle isn't you at all? What happens when other people's opinions, expectations, and reactions start carrying more weight than your purpose?

Those questions we will evaluate and answer in the next chapter.

Catch it. Challenge it. Commit.

CHAPTER 14

When "I Got It" Keeps You Alone

"Carrying it alone feels strong until it starts breaking you."

Sometimes "I got it" can sound like confidence, but it can also be the sentence that keeps you alone. Carrying everything by yourself can look like strength, until it becomes your ceiling.

The issue isn't that you're capable. The issue is that your capability has started replacing trust, partnership, and support. Somewhere along the way, you learned it felt safer to handle it yourself than to risk being disappointed, let down, or exposed.

But that way of living comes with a cost. You stay productive, but you get isolated. You keep building, but you keep bleeding in private. Research tells us why. A large meta-analysis found that people with stronger social relationships had a significantly higher likelihood of survival over time than people with weaker relationships. In plain language, connection is not just emotional comfort. It is a health and sustainability factor, which is why isolation eventually starts costing more than it saves.[42] As you read this chapter, we will break the belief that you have to do everything alone to make sure it gets done right. You'll also learn how to let support in without losing your standards, and how to build what matters without carrying the whole weight by yourself. This is where the TSM Loop becomes practical. You have to catch the "I got it" thought, challenge the story underneath it, and commit to letting support in one rung at a time.

THE CHALLENGE OF LETTING GO

I must be honest. If I'm not honest, nobody is transformed.

Hyper-independence has been one of the biggest battles in my mind. And if I had to define it, I'd say it like this: hyper-independence is the habit of carrying everything alone because trusting support feels unsafe. Attachment research helps explain why this feels so automatic. Studies on support-seeking in close relationships found that avoidant attachment predicts less effective support seeking, meaning some people instinctively pull back, minimize needs, or carry them alone, even when support is available.[43] That lines up with what you're describing. Sometimes "I got it" is not confidence. It's a learned way to stay unhurt. Not unsafe like danger in the street, unsafe like disappointment. Unsafe like letting someone touch something you care about and watching them mishandle it.

I've lived long enough to know what it feels like to give someone a task, to share a piece of your vision, to hand them a piece of you, and later realize they didn't hold it the way you hold it. They didn't give it the same attention. They didn't carry the weight of it the same way. And over time, that pain can harden into a belief that sounds responsible but is really restrictive:

"If I don't do it, it won't get done right."

I've felt that. I've lived that.

Even when I launched my businesses, I asked people for help. They said they would step in, and then they didn't. It created a letdown, and that letdown turned into proof in my mind. My thoughts started talking to me like they were protecting me: *See? You were right. You can't trust people to help you the way you need help.*

So I kept shouldering things. Weekends. Weekdays. Late nights. Early mornings. I gave up rest because I didn't feel safe handing the torch to anyone else. And the truth is, it wore me down. Not all at once, but slowly.

Because purpose is heavy. Vision is heavy. Building anything meaningful is heavy. And when you're the only one carrying it, eventually the weight starts changing you. You become tired, guarded, and resentful, even if you're still productive. That's how

> **Asking for help is not weakness.**
> **It is strategy.**

hyper-independence sneaks in. It doesn't always start as pride. Most of the time, it starts as protection.

It's like carrying a baby. You nurture it. You grow it. You protect it. You carry it for months. And when it's finally time to give birth to what you've been building, you want someone else to nurture it the way you do.

But when you don't believe anyone will, you keep it in your arms forever.

And you wonder why you're tired.

THE MIND TRAP

Hyper-independence is when you confuse control with safety, and you carry everything alone because trust feels risky.

It keeps you busy, but it keeps you alone.

People praised me for it. They called it dedication. They called it work ethic. They had no idea what it was costing me.

But I was exhausted. I was holding weight that was never meant for one person. And I had done it so long I forgot there was another way. Then I started practicing trust in small doses. Not with my whole vision. Just one piece at a time. The question isn't whether you can carry it. You can.

The question is what it is costing you, and whether you're willing to build support that doesn't require you to bleed first.

WHY THIS HAPPENS

Hyper-independence does not come from arrogance. It comes from experience.

Past letdowns when support did not show up. You asked for help once. Maybe more than once. And people let you down. They forgot. They half-delivered. They did not care like you cared. That disappointment became a lesson: do not count on people.

High personal standards and deep care for the vision. You are not just being difficult. You genuinely care about how your work is done. When something has your name on it, you want it done well. And trusting someone else with that standard feels like a risk.

Fear of things crumbling if you hand them off. What if they mess it up? What if you have to redo it anyway? What if letting go of control means watching something you built fall apart? That fear keeps you holding on.

Control as a way to survive. When you have been let down enough times, control starts feeling like the only thing you can count on. If you manage every piece, nothing can surprise you. Nothing can disappoint you. But that control comes at a cost.

Difficulty trusting others with what is tied to your purpose. You can delegate a task. But can you delegate a piece of your calling? When the work is personal, handing it off feels vulnerable. And vulnerability is not where hyper-independence likes to live.

Resentment from previous letdowns that became proof. Every time someone failed to show up, your mind filed it away as evidence. *See? This is why I do things myself.* That evidence now runs the show, even when new people might be different.

THE COST

Hyper-independence does not protect your vision. It shrinks it.

Burnout and exhaustion become your baseline. You are not resting because you cannot afford to rest. Every task feels urgent because you are the only one who can do it. That pace does not announce when it is too much. It just breaks you quietly.

Your progress gets delayed because one person has limits. You can only do so much in a day. You can only scale so far alone. The very thing you built to protect your vision becomes the ceiling that keeps it small.

You carry isolation and emotional heaviness. When you do not let people in, you hold not only the tasks but the weight of doing it alone. That heaviness builds. You get guarded. You get irritable. And even when people are around, you feel alone.

You cannot scale your business, platform, or purpose work. Growth requires systems. Systems require people. And if you cannot trust people, your growth has a ceiling you built yourself.

You hold resentment toward people who never agreed to carry what you never clearly asked them to carry. Sometimes the disappointment is not their failure. It is a missed conversation, an unclear expectation, or an ask you never actually made out loud.

THINK SHIFT: THE TRUST LADDER (CATCH IT)

Here is what helped me when I realized I was carrying too much.

The Tool: The Trust Ladder

You do not go from "I do everything" to "I trust everyone." You climb.

The Trust Ladder has four rungs:

Rung 1: Task I can delegate with low risk.

Start with something that matters but will not devastate you if it is not perfect. Not your keynote. Not your flagship offer. Something smaller.

Rung 2: Clear standard for what done means.

Write it down. What does success look like for this task? Be specific. Vague asks create vague results.

Rung 3: Short timeline plus check-in.

Do not hand it off and disappear. Set a deadline. Schedule a check-in. This is not micromanaging. It is building trust through visibility. Why is this true? Well, in team research, psychological safety is described as a shared belief that it's safe to take interpersonal risks, like asking questions, admitting uncertainty, or requesting help. When psychological safety is higher, people learn faster and speak up more. Your ladder is doing something powerful. It's reducing the relational risk one rung at a time.[44]

Rung 4: Review outcome, not method.

When the task is done, evaluate what matters: did it meet the standard? If yes, it does not matter that they did it differently than you would have. Let go of method. Hold onto outcome.

Start with one rung this week. The goal is not to hand off your whole life. The goal is to prove to your mind that support can be safe again.

When to use it: When you feel overwhelmed but cannot imagine handing anything off. When you catch yourself saying "I will just do it myself." When your to-do list is longer than your energy.

How long it takes: Five minutes to identify the task and write the standard. The rest happens over the week.

What it produces: A low-risk way to practice trusting others. Evidence that delegation can work. Breathing room.

Reflection Questions:

1. What am I afraid will happen if I ask for help?
2. Is my standard clarity, or is it perfection?
3. What is one thing I can hand off without putting my whole vision at risk?

SPEAK SHIFT: THE SUPPORT SCRIPT (CHALLENGE IT)

The way I talk to myself about help either keeps me carrying alone or opens the door to support. I had to change the script.

Here are the phrases I stopped saying:

I'll just do it myself.

Nobody will do it right.

It's easier if I handle it.

I don't want to be disappointed.

I can't trust people.

Here is what I started saying instead:

I do not need perfect help. I need real support.

Trust can be built in small steps.

My purpose deserves a team.

I can set standards without carrying everything.

Asking for help is not weakness. It is strategy.

Speak the Truth (Reframe): What is the honest sentence I need to say out loud to invite support with clarity?

Example starter: "Here's what I need, here's what done looks like, and here's when I need it by."

Now write yours:_____

Commit doesn't mean trusting everyone. It means building support on purpose.

MANIFEST SHIFT: THE DELEGATION BOUNDARY PLAN (COMMIT)

Hyper-independence loses its grip when you create clear boundaries around what you carry, what you share, and what you release. This plan helps you shift from holding everything to building a sustainable support structure.

WHEN "I GOT IT" KEEPS YOU ALONE

What Changes

Identify 3 to 5 tasks you have been shouldering that someone else could handle. These are tasks that do not require your unique expertise. They matter, but they do not need to be done by you.

Examples:

- Scheduling and calendar management
- Social media posting (not strategy, just execution)
- Email sorting and first-response drafts
- Research and information gathering
- Event planning and coordination

What Stays

Identify the tasks that truly require you. These are the things tied to your voice, your vision, your unique contribution. Protect these. Do not delegate what only you can do.

Examples:

- Writing your content and messaging
- Speaking and presenting
- Strategic decisions about your platform
- Relationships that require your personal presence

What Stops

Identify the habits and patterns that keep you carrying alone. These are the behaviors, not tasks. Name them so you can interrupt them.

Examples:

- Saying "I will just do it myself" before considering alternatives

- Redoing tasks instead of giving clear feedback
- Assuming people will fail before they have tried
- Holding resentment instead of having conversations

Write this plan down. Review it weekly. Let it guide your decisions about what to carry and what to release.

QUICK EXERCISE: THE BODY CHECK

This exercise takes about 10 minutes and helps you notice how hyper-independence shows up in your body, not just your mind. It helps you catch the pattern before it turns into burnout. Best used when you keep saying "I'm fine" but your body is tense, heavy, or exhausted—and you know you're carrying too much.

Step 1: Sit Quietly for Two Minutes

Close your eyes. Breathe slow. Pay attention to what your body is holding.

Step 2: Find Where You Are Holding the Weight

Ask yourself: Where do I feel the weight of carrying everything? Common places include:

- Shoulders (carrying responsibility)
- Jaw (holding tension, not speaking needs)
- Chest (guarded, protecting)
- Stomach (anxiety about letting go)
- Back (supporting weight alone)

Step 3: Name What It Is Protecting

Ask yourself: What is this tension trying to protect me from? Write your answer.

Example: "My shoulders are tight because I am afraid that if I let go, things will fall apart."

Step 4: Speak a Release

Say out loud or write:

- "I do not have to carry this alone."
- "I can ask for support without losing control."

Use this exercise when you feel physically drained, when your body is holding tension you can't explain, or when you need a reminder that carrying everything is not the only option.

OUTCOME EVIDENCE

After practicing these tools, you should notice:

- At least one delegated task completed by someone else
- Reduced overload and increased breathing room
- Clearer standards and communication around expectations
- Less resentment and more willingness to ask for support
- A written plan distinguishing what you carry, what you share, and what you release

CONCLUDING THOUGHTS

I used to think carrying everything alone made me strong. I thought it proved my dedication, my work ethic, my ability to handle whatever came my way.

But strength that isolates you is not sustainable. And dedication that burns you out is not wisdom.

The truth I had to face was that hyper-independence was not protecting my vision. It was limiting it. The very control I held so tightly was the ceiling keeping everything small. And the disappointment I was trying to avoid? I was creating it myself by never letting anyone fully in.

Your vision needs more than one set of hands. Not perfect people. Not people who carry things exactly like you. But real support, built in small steps, with clear standards and room to grow together.

Asking for help is not weakness. It is strategy. And it might be the next step your vision has been waiting for. Catch it. Challenge it. Commit.

How To Move Forward

You now have tools for releasing hyper-independence. You know how to climb the Trust Ladder and build a support structure around your vision. But what happens when the obstacle is not about carrying alone? What happens when the obstacle is about what other people think?

When their opinions, expectations, or reactions have more power over your decisions than your own purpose does? Let's focus on how to answer these questions next.

CHAPTER 15

The Shame Loop

"Healing starts when the thing you hid finally has a name."

Shame doesn't just remind you of what happened. It rewrites what it means about you. It keeps you silent, isolates you, and convinces you that freedom is for other people. In this chapter, we're going to name what's been buried so your healing finally has somewhere to begin.

Many people don't realize this: across trauma-exposed populations (including survivors of childhood abuse or neglect, intimate partner violence, sexual assault, and community violence), shame is consistently linked with higher posttraumatic stress symptoms. In one meta-analysis of 25 studies, the association was moderate and reliable, which means shame is not a side note. It often becomes part of what keeps the wound active.[45]

What happens when what you're carrying isn't a task or a responsibility, but something from your past you've never spoken out loud? When the weight isn't about what you need to do, but about what happened to you?

And that's the trap we're confronting here: the cycle that keeps you buried–punishing yourself in silence, rehearsing fear, and calling it protection when it's really a prison.

Let's take a moment to look at how shame influences our conversations and recognize that it all starts in the mind. If this chapter touches something tender, take your time. Pause when you need to, breathe, and come back when you're ready. You're safe here—and you're not alone.

This is where the TSM Loop becomes a lifeline. You catch the shame story as it rises, you challenge what it's trying to make "true" about you, and you commit to one safe step toward

> **Healing cannot happen in hiding forever.**

release. Not exposure. Release.

THE VULNERABLE AUTHOR

I recently had a conversation with someone about a friend who wrote a book but never told people close to him what he had really been through.

The best friend felt hurt. Like, *if I'm your best friend, I should know everything about you.*

And I get that feeling. I do.

But I also know another side of the truth.

There are things that are easy to talk about, and then there are things that are traumatic. Things that replay in your mind. Things you bury. Things you hide because you do not know how people will respond, and you do not want to risk being judged for something that already wounded you.

THE SHAME LOOP

In *Oakland Hills, Milwaukee Rivers*, in the chapter "Silent Shadows," I reveal something that happened to me as a child. I did not talk about it for decades. I hid it.

I hid it because it happened so long ago and I did not know how to share it. I feared judgment. I feared people asking the wrong questions and calling it concern.

Why didn't you tell somebody?

Why didn't you stop it?

Why didn't you run?

Why didn't you fight back?

Why didn't you say something sooner?

Questions like that can feel like a second injury. Especially when someone does not understand how trauma works in real life. Studies on disclosure show that negative social reactions (like disbelief, blame, or harsh questioning) are associated with greater psychological distress and trauma symptoms, while supportive responses relate to healthier adjustment. So when you call it a second injury, you're not being dramatic. You're describing a pattern clinicians have documented for years.[46] Sometimes we do not share because we are afraid we will not be believed. Sometimes we do not share because we fear people will judge us like we contributed to what happened to us.[47]

So I tucked it into my subconscious. I kept living. I kept functioning. But the memory did not disappear. It would surface from time to time, and I learned how to push it back down.

And there was another layer too.

I knew that moment could be connected to how I understood my identity and my sexuality. That alone made me avoid it even more. Because shame does not just hide a moment. It hides the meaning you are afraid people will attach to it.

Eventually I decided to write it. Not for shock. Not for sympathy.

I wrote it because I was tired of carrying a secret that kept showing up in my mind like it still owned me. I wrote it because I needed to face it. Because healing cannot happen in hiding forever.

That is what shame loops do. They punish you in private. They make you rehearse fear. They keep you silent. And they convince you silence is safety.

But silence is not safety. It is a cell. Silence feels like control, but it becomes captivity when it's fueled by fear.

THE MIND TRAP

Shame loops are cycles where fear of judgment leads to hiding, which then leads to isolation, and then isolation leads to self-punishment.

It keeps you stuck in your own head.

Here is how it works. Something wounds you. Shame wraps around it. You hide it to stay safe. But the hiding does not make it go away. It just moves underground, replaying in your mind, surfacing when you least expect it, making you feel like the wound is still fresh even years later.

And because I never let it out, I never got to hear what I needed to hear. Shame kept me trapped with a private version of the story, one where judgment was guaranteed and safety only existed in silence. You never get to find out that the judgment you feared may not be as universal as you imagined. You don't get to receive compassion, perspective, or truth. You just keep replaying the wound with shame as the narrator.

WHY THIS HAPPENS

Shame loops do not come from weakness. They come from self-protection that got stuck on repeat.

For a lot of people, the first fear is not even judgment. It's disbelief. You don't know how someone will respond, and that uncertainty can feel dangerous. What if they question your story? What if they look at you differently after they know? What if they don't believe you at all? Sometimes that fear alone is enough to keep you silent for years.

Then there is the fear of being blamed. The fear that someone will take your wound and turn it into a courtroom. Why didn't you do something different. Why didn't you stop it. Why didn't you say something sooner. Shame convinces you that people will think you caused what happened to you, or that you should have been able to prevent it. And that kind of fear makes hiding feel like the smartest option.

And let's be honest, sometimes you're not trying to hide because you're weak. You're trying to avoid being seen as weak. You don't want pity. You don't want to be treated like you're fragile or broken. So you perform strength. You keep functioning. You keep producing. But that performance gets exhausting, because you're carrying something heavy while pretending it's light.

Another layer is reaction. You can't control what people say when you tell them. You can't control their face, their tone, their follow-up questions, or whether they handle your truth with care. So your mind decides it's safer to avoid the whole thing than to risk being wounded twice.

And even when you bury it, the mind doesn't forget just because you don't talk about it. The memory stays. It surfaces at random. And every time it does, you push it back down instead of letting it move through you. That is how the loop stays alive.

Sometimes there is one more layer that makes it even harder to speak. Identity shame. Not just fear about what happened, but fear about what people will conclude about who you are because of it. That layer can feel like exposure. It can feel like losing control of your own story. And when shame convinces you that being seen will cost you everything, silence starts feeling like the only place you can breathe.

If you want a final closing line to seal this section before the exercise, add this: Shame is not proof something is wrong. It's proof you've been trying to survive.

THE COST

Shame loops do not protect you. They imprison you.

Your healing gets delayed. The wound that could have started closing years ago stays open because you never let air reach it. You carry it silently, and the weight of that silence compounds over time.

You stay isolated. The people closest to you may know something is off, but they do not know what. And because you do not tell them, they cannot show up for you in the way you actually need.

Your relationships become guarded. Closeness requires honesty. But when you have been hiding for years, filtering becomes automatic. Even people who love you only get part of you. So even in close relationships, part of you stays hidden.

The painful moment keeps replaying. You think you buried it, but it keeps coming back. A song. A smell. A comment someone makes. And suddenly you are right back there, feeling everything again.

You live smaller to avoid exposure. You pass on opportunities, avoid certain conversations, and steer clear of situations where the truth might come out. Your world shrinks to protect a secret that no longer needs protecting.

THINK SHIFT: NAME IT WITHOUT BLAME (CATCH IT)

Here is what helped me when shame kept me silent. If you're not ready to tell the whole story, don't. Start smaller. Tell the truth to one safe place—your journal, your therapist, God, or one trusted person who has earned access to you. Your focus isn't exposure. It's release.

The Tool: Name It Without Blaming Yourself

Shame stays alive when you keep it unnamed and in the dark. This is why naming it matters. Research on emotional disclosure, including structured writing about painful experiences, shows small but reliable benefits for psychological and physical well-being across many studies. And when you pair truth-telling with compassion, outcomes can improve even more.[48] A compassion-based intervention study found meaningful reductions in trauma-related shame and PTSD symptoms, which fits the spirit of what you're building here: truth without self-destruction. The first step toward breaking its grip is to name what happened clearly, without taking on blame that does not belong to you.

Write two sentences:

Think. Speak. Manifest.

Sentence 1: "What happened was..." (Write the facts only. No interpretation. No self-blame. Just what occurred.)

Sentence 2: "What I needed then was..." (Name what the younger version of you needed: compassion, protection, belief, support, safety.)

Example:

- *What happened was someone I trusted crossed a line when I was a child.*
- *What I needed then was protection, belief, and someone to tell me it was not my fault.*

You are not reliving it. You are finally putting words to it. And words take some of the power back. When you call it out, it loses some of its power over you. When you name what you needed, you start to give yourself the compassion you have been withholding.

When to use it: When a memory keeps surfacing. When you feel shame but cannot explain why. When you are carrying something you have never spoken out loud.

How long it takes: Five minutes. Just two sentences. You can go deeper later if you choose.

What it produces: Clarity. Self-compassion. A shift from self-blame to honest acknowledgment.

Reflection Questions:
1. Who taught me I should be ashamed of this?
2. What part of me is still trying to stay safe?
3. What would I tell a child who went through what I went through?

SPEAK SHIFT: THE VOICE OF SHAME (CHALLENGE IT)

Shame has a voice. It whispers things you would never say to someone you love. I had to learn to interrupt that voice and replace it with truth.

Here are the phrases I stopped agreeing with:

I should have said something.

People will judge me.

They won't believe me.

I'm going to look weak.

It's my fault.

Here is what I started saying instead:

What happened to me is not who I am.

Silence protected me then, but it will not heal me now.

I can share at my pace and still be free.

I do not need everyone to understand for my healing to be real.

I am not guilty for my past.

Speak the Truth (out loud or on paper):

Finish this sentence without explaining or apologizing:

"What happened to me was not my fault, and what I need now is _____."

(Examples: support, space, clarity, counseling, prayer, a conversation, time, gentleness, permission to heal.)

"The next safe step I can take is _____."

MANIFEST SHIFT: THE THREE-STEP SHIFT (COMMIT)

Breaking a shame loop is not about telling everyone everything all at once. It is about moving from silence to intentional release, one step at a time. Commit means you stop partnering with silence. You choose one safe outlet and one honest step.

Step 1: Notice

Pay attention to when shame shows up. It often arrives as a sudden wave of discomfort, a memory that surfaces, or a reflexive urge to hide. Notice it without judging yourself for it.

Ask yourself: *What just got triggered? What am I feeling right now?*

Step 2: Name

Use the "Name It Without Blaming Yourself" tool. Write the two sentences. Get clear on what happened and what you needed. Naming the thing takes it out of the shadows.

Ask yourself: *What is the truth of what happened? What compassion do I owe myself?*

Step 3: Next

Choose one safe outlet for the next layer of release. This is not about dumping your entire story on the first person available. It is about choosing wisely and moving intentionally.

Safe outlets include:
- A private journal entry

- A trusted person who has earned the right to hear your story
- A counselor or support professional
- A support group or safe community resource

Ask yourself: *What is one safe step I can take toward release this week?*

You do not have to share the whole story at once. Share one layer. See how it feels. Healing does not have a deadline. Move at your speed.

QUICK EXERCISE: THE SHAME LOOP REPLAY

This exercise takes about 10 minutes and helps you process a memory that keeps resurfacing instead of pushing it back down. This helps you separate what happened from what shame keeps telling you it means.

Step 1: Identify the Trigger

Think of a recent moment when shame surfaced. What triggered it? A conversation? A memory? A comment someone made?

Write: "The moment that triggered me was..."

Step 2: Name the Story You Told Yourself

What did your mind say in that moment? What shame-based narrative kicked in?

Write: "The story I told myself was..."

Step 3: Name What You Actually Needed

What did you need in that moment, if you can name it? What do you need now?

Write: "What I actually needed was…..."

Step 4: Choose Your Next Step

Your next step does not have to be public. It just has to be honest.

What is one thing you can do this week to move toward release instead of stuffing it back down?

Write: "A safe next step for me is…"

Use this exercise any time a memory surfaces and you feel the pull to hide. Let it move through you instead of staying stuck inside you.

OUTCOME EVIDENCE

After practicing these tools, you should notice:

- Less self-blame language in how you think and speak about yourself.
- At least one intentional step toward release (writing, sharing, or seeking support).
- More kindness toward yourself when memories surface.
- Fewer spirals and less power when they come.
- A clearer understanding that what happened to you is not who you are.

A NOTE BEFORE YOU CONTINUE

If this chapter stirred something heavy, you don't have to carry it alone. Getting support—therapy, pastoral care, a trusted counselor, or a safe group—isn't weakness. It's wisdom. A counselor or therapist can help you work through what you have been carrying. You do not have to figure this out alone. You do not have to do this by yourself.

Healing at your pace is still healing. And asking for help is part of the process.

CLOSING

I hid something for 30 years. Not because I wanted to, but because I didn't know how to explain it–and I feared what people would conclude about me if they knew.

Then I wrote it down. Not to shock anyone or seek pity, but because I was tired of letting a secret own me. Healing can't happen in hiding forever.

You don't have to tell the whole world, and you don't have to share before you're ready. But you do need to start naming it, even if only to yourself–because shame dies in the light, and what stays hidden stays heavy.

What happened to you is not who you are. Silence protected you then, but it won't heal you now. The thing you tucked away deserves a name. And so does your freedom..

The Power to Move Forward

You now have tools for breaking shame loops and moving from silence to intentional release. You know how to name what happened without blaming yourself and how to take safe steps toward healing.

But what happens when the obstacle isn't something from your past, it's something in your present? When you already know what to do, but procrastination keeps winning and the gap between intention and action keeps widening? This is where we go next to strengthen comprehension.

Catch it. Challenge it. Commit.

SHIFT CHECK

Pause. Reflect. Notice the shift.

Focus: Shame, self-protection, and the courage to be seen

THINK (Catch it): Patterns I'm Becoming Aware Of

What past moment or mistake do I keep returning to when I think about who I am?

_____

_____

Where have I been punishing myself for something I have already survived?

_____

_____

SPEAK (Challenge it): Scripts I'm Interrupting

What do I keep telling myself about what I deserve based on where I have been?

_____

_____

What phrase do I use to convince myself that healing or wholeness is not for me?

_____

_____

Speak the Truth (Reframe): What is the truth I need to speak back to that script, even if I don't feel it yet?

The truth is:

_____

_____

MANIFEST (Commit): Evidence of Movement

Where did I extend grace to myself this week instead of judgment?

_____

_____

What did I forgive myself for, or at least loosen my grip on?

_____

_____

MANIFEST (Commit): Recommitment

What part of my story am I ready to stop hiding from?

_____

_____

CONCLUSION

The Lock and the Key

"A lock does two things. It protects what's valuable, and it restricts what has access."

As we close this book, I want to leave you with something personal. A couple of years ago, I bought a silver necklace with a small lock pendant—just a simple padlock with a keyhole. I wasn't looking for a life lesson. I was just buying a piece. But later, I realized I had purchased something symbolic—something I didn't even know I needed.

But later, I realized I had purchased something symbolic—something I didn't even know I needed—because that lock started reminding me of how life works. Let's bring it home and make it practical.

A lock does two things: it protects what's valuable, and it restricts what has access. It can keep something secure, or keep something contained. Either way, nothing changes until the person with the key decides it's time.

And that's what hit me: the only person who can unlock that necklace is me. I'm the one who takes it off. I'm the one who protects it. I'm the one who decides what it means and what it represents. Nobody else can come into my life and unlock what I'm wearing.

That's how your life works too.

Think. Speak. Manifest.

Your potential is valuable. Your dreams matter. Your future is worth protecting. Your opportunities are real. And so often, it's all sitting behind an internal "lock"—not because the goal isn't possible, but because your mind has decided it feels safer to keep it closed than to risk what happens when you open it.

That's why we've talked so much in this book about mastering the mind. If you've made it here, I want you to sit with one truth: a lot of what has been heavy in your life wasn't heavy because it was impossible. It was heavy because you kept carrying it in your mind first.

For many of us, the real battle was never just the situation. It was the story we kept attaching to it. The meaning we gave it. The fear we kept feeding. The opinions we kept letting sit in the driver's seat. And the longer you let that happen, the more your life starts shrinking around what feels "safe."

But safe isn't always safe.

Sometimes it's just fear with better marketing.

Let me ask you something that matters more than any chapter in this book: how much of your life has been shaped by things you can't control—other people's reactions, other people's moods, other people's opinions—when the power has been in your hands the whole time?

People will do what they do. They'll misunderstand you. They'll project. They'll clap one day and question you the next. Opinions shift. Rooms change. The "weather" of life is always moving. The difference now is that you don't have to move with it.

You get to decide what gets access to you. You get to decide what gets to shape you. You get to decide what gets the final word. That's what reclaiming your power really looks like.

THE LOCK AND THE KEY

This doesn't mean you never feel fear again. It means fear stops making decisions for you. It means you stop rehearsing worst-case outcomes like they're prophecy. It means you stop hiding your ability, your voice, your work, your calling—because you finally understand the cost of staying silent.

You've already paid that cost long enough.

What I want you to remember when you close this book is simple: your mind is not just where thoughts happen. It's where permission happens. It's where you either agree with purpose or argue with it. It's where you decide if you will keep waiting for certainty, or if you will move with what you already know.

And the reason I built this book around **Think. Speak. Manifest.** is because those three aren't just a title—they're a pattern you can live by. And when your mind starts spiraling again—which it will—you don't have to negotiate with it. You can run the loop: catch it, challenge it, commit.

Think: What you repeatedly tell yourself becomes a blueprint. If your thinking is filled with delay, defeat, and doubt, your life will start matching that script. But if your thinking is grounded in truth, clarity, and purpose, you start moving differently.

Speak: Your words are either reinforcement or resistance. They either train your mind toward courage or keep your fear on life support. What you say—especially when you're under pressure—matters more than you realize.

Manifest: Your future doesn't come from intention alone. It comes from movement. From consistency. From choices that exist outside your head. Because the antidote isn't more thinking. It's movement.

Here's my challenge to you, and I mean it with love: don't let this become something you agree with but never apply. Pick one

Think. Speak. Manifest.

area—just one—where you've been overthinking, shrinking, delaying, or waiting for permission.

Write down the thought that keeps locking the door. Replace it with what's true. Speak it out loud without apologizing. Then take one step—today—that proves fear isn't in charge anymore.

Make the phone call. Send the email. Submit the application. Start the plan. Set the boundary. Write the page. Do the thing you keep circling around.

Just move.

Because the door only stays locked if you let it.

And that lock necklace? I wear it differently now. It reminds me that what's valuable should be protected—but not imprisoned. It reminds me that I am responsible for what I carry, what I believe, what I speak, and what I choose to open.

Your potential isn't waiting on the world to change. It's waiting on you to turn the key.

Now go unlock what's been in you the whole time. Keep walking it out—one choice at a time.

End Notes

1. Steel, Piers. "The Nature of Procrastination: A Meta-Analytic and Theoretical Review of Quintessential Self-Regulatory Failure." *Psychological Bulletin* 133, no. 1 (2007): 65–94. https://doi.org/10.1037/0033-2909.133.1.65.

2. Newman, Michelle G., and Sandra J. Llera. "A Novel Theory of Experiential Avoidance in Generalized Anxiety Disorder: A Review and Synthesis of Research Supporting a Contrast Avoidance Model of Worry." *Clinical Psychology Review* 31, no. 3 (2011): 371–382. https://doi.org/10.1016/j.cpr.2011.01.008.

3. Feinstein, Brian A. "The Rejection Sensitivity Model as a Framework for Understanding Sexual Minority Mental Health." *Archives of Sexual Behavior* 49, no. 7 (2020): 2247–2258. https://doi.org/10.1007/s10508-019-1428-3. (Epub July 8, 2019.)

4. Ragins, Belle Rose, Romila Singh, and John M. Cornwell. "Making the Invisible Visible: Fear and Disclosure of Sexual Orientation at Work." *Journal of Applied Psychology* 92, no. 4 (2007): 1103–1118. https://doi.org/10.1037/0021-9010.92.4.1103.

5. Leigh, Eleanor, Kenny Chiu, and David M. Clark. "Self-Focused Attention and Safety Behaviours Maintain Social Anxiety in Adolescents: An Experimental Study." *PLOS ONE* 16, no. 2 (2021): e0247703. https://doi.org/10.1371/journal.pone.0247703.

6. Adamska, Krystyna, and Paweł Jurek. "Come and Say What You Think: Reducing Employees' Self-Censorship through Procedural and Interpersonal Justice." *Current Issues in Personality Psychology* 9, no. 4 (2021): 328–340. https://doi.org/10.5114/cipp.2021.110022.

7. Ragins, Belle Rose, Romila Singh, and John M. Cornwell. "Making the Invisible Visible: Fear and Disclosure of Sexual Orientation at Work." *Journal of Applied Psychology* 92, no. 4 (2007): 1103–1118. https://doi.org/10.1037/0021-9010.92.4.1103.

8. Newman, Michelle G., and Sandra J. Llera. "A Novel Theory of Experiential Avoidance in Generalized Anxiety Disorder: A Review and Synthesis of Research Supporting a Contrast Avoidance Model of Worry." *Clinical Psychology Review* 31, no. 3 (2011): 371–382. https://doi.org/10.1016/j.cpr.2011.01.008.

9. Crocker, Jennifer, and Connie T. Wolfe. "Contingencies of Self-Worth." *Psychological Review* 108, no. 3 (2001): 593–623. https://doi.org/10.1037/0033-295X.108.3.593.

10. Hill, Andrew P., and Thomas Curran. "Multidimensional Perfectionism and Burnout: A Meta-Analysis." *Personality and Social Psychology Review* 20, no. 3 (2016): 269–288. https://doi.org/10.1177/1088868315596286.

11. Steel, Piers. "The Nature of Procrastination: A Meta-Analytic and Theoretical Review of Quintessential Self-Regulatory Failure." *Psychological Bulletin* 133, no. 1 (2007): 65–94. https://doi.org/10.1037/0033-2909.133.1.65.

12. Einstein, Danielle A. "Extension of the Transdiagnostic Model to Focus on Intolerance of Uncertainty: A Review of the Literature and Implications for Treatment." *Clinical*

Psychology: Science and Practice 21, no. 3 (2014): 280-300. https://doi.org/10.1111/cpsp.12077.

13. Gollwitzer, Peter M., and Paschal Sheeran. "Implementation Intentions and Goal Achievement: A Meta-Analysis of Effects and Processes." *Advances in Experimental Social Psychology* 38 (2006): 69-119.

14. Jack, Dana C., and Diane Dill. "The Silencing the Self Scale: Schemas of Intimacy Associated with Depression in Women." *Psychology of Women Quarterly* 16, no. 1 (1992): 97-106. https://doi.org/10.1111/j.1471-6402.1992.tb00242.x.

15. Pinder, Craig C., and Karen P. Harlos. "Employee Silence: Quiescence and Acquiescence as Responses to Perceived Injustice." *Research in Personnel and Human Resources Management* 20 (2001): 331-369. https://doi.org/10.1016/S0742-7301(01)20007-3.

16. Speed, Brittany C., Brittany L. Goldstein, and Marvin R. Goldfried. "Assertiveness Training: A Forgotten Evidence-Based Treatment." *Clinical Psychology: Science and Practice* 25 (2018): e12216. https://doi.org/10.1111/cpsp.12216.

17. Festinger, Leon. "A Theory of Social Comparison Processes." *Human Relations* 7, no. 2 (1954): 117-140. https://doi.org/10.1177/001872675400700202.

18. Vogel, Erin A., Jason P. Rose, Lindsay R. Roberts, and Katheryn Eckles. "Social Comparison, Social Media, and Self-Esteem." *Psychology of Popular Media Culture* 3, no. 4 (2014): 206-222. https://doi.org/10.1037/ppm0000047.

19. Kross, Ethan, Philippe Verduyn, Emre Demiralp, Jiyoung Park, David S. Lee, Natalie Lin, et al. "Facebook Use Predicts Declines in Subjective Well-Being in Young Adults." *PLOS*

ONE 8, no. 8 (2013): e69841. https://doi.org/10.1371/journal.pone.0069841.

20. Lally, Phillippa, Cornelia H. M. van Jaarsveld, Henry W. W. Potts, and Jane Wardle. "How Are Habits Formed: Modelling Habit Formation in the Real World." *European Journal of Social Psychology* 40, no. 6 (2010): 998–1009. https://doi.org/10.1002/ejsp.674.

21. Sirois, Fuschia M., Dora S. Molnar, and James K. Hirsch. "A Meta-Analytic and Conceptual Update on the Associations between Procrastination and Multidimensional Perfectionism." *Personality and Individual Differences* 108 (2017): 1–6. https://doi.org/10.1016/j.paid.2016.12.033.

22. Limburg, Katja, Hunna J. Watson, Martin S. Hagger, and Sarah J. Egan. "The Relationship between Perfectionism and Psychopathology: A Meta-Analysis." *Journal of Clinical Psychology* 73, no. 10 (2017): 1301–1326. https://doi.org/10.1002/jclp.22435.

23. Hill, Andrew P., and Thomas Curran. "Multidimensional Perfectionism and Burnout: A Meta-Analysis." *Personality and Social Psychology Review* 20, no. 3 (2016): 269–288. https://doi.org/10.1177/1088868315596286.

24. Bravata, D. M., S. A. Watts, A. L. Keefer, et al. "Prevalence, Predictors, and Treatment of Impostor Syndrome: A Systematic Review." *Journal of General Internal Medicine* 35, no. 4 (2020): 1252–1275. https://doi.org/10.1007/s11606-019-05364-1.

25. Schmader, Toni, Michael Johns, and Chad Forbes. "An Integrated Process Model of Stereotype Threat Effects on Performance." *Psychological Review* 115, no. 2 (2008): 336–356. https://doi.org/10.1037/0033-295X.115.2.336.

END NOTES

26. Ezawa, Iony D., and Steven D. Hollon. "Cognitive Restructuring and Psychotherapy Outcome: A Meta-Analytic Review." *Psychotherapy* 60, no. 3 (2023): 396–406. https://doi.org/10.1037/pst0000474.

27. Gellatly, R., and Aaron T. Beck. "Catastrophic Thinking: A Transdiagnostic Process across Psychiatric Disorders." *Cognitive Therapy and Research* 40 (2016): 441–452. https://doi.org/10.1007/s10608-016-9763-3.

28. Nolen-Hoeksema, Susan, Blair E. Wisco, and Sonja Lyubomirsky. "Rethinking Rumination." *Perspectives on Psychological Science* 3, no. 5 (2008): 400–424. https://doi.org/10.1111/j.1745-6924.2008.00088.x.

29. Scullin, Michael K., Michelle L. Krueger, Hannah K. Ballard, Nicole Pruett, and Donald L. Bliwise. "The Effects of Bedtime Writing on Difficulty Falling Asleep: A Polysomnographic Study Comparing To-Do Lists and Completed Activity Lists." *Journal of Experimental Psychology: General* 147, no. 1 (2018): 139–146. https://doi.org/10.1037/xge0000374.

30. Al-Mosaiwi, Mohammad, and Tom Johnstone. "In an Absolute State: Elevated Use of Absolutist Words Is a Marker Specific to Anxiety, Depression, and Suicidal Ideation." *Clinical Psychological Science* 6, no. 4 (2018): 529–542. https://doi.org/10.1177/2167702617747074

31. Dweck, Carol S., and Ellen L. Leggett. "A Social-Cognitive Approach to Motivation and Personality." *Psychological Review* 95, no. 2 (1988): 256–273. https://doi.org/10.1037/0033-295X.95.2.256.

32. Breines, Juliana G., and Serena Chen. "Self-Compassion Increases Self-Improvement Motivation." *Personality and*

Social Psychology Bulletin 38, no. 9 (2012): 1133–1143. https://doi.org/10.1177/0146167212445599.

33. Stajkovic, Alexander D., and Fred Luthans. "Self-Efficacy and Work-Related Performance: A Meta-Analysis." *Psychological Bulletin* 124, no. 2 (1998): 240–261. https://doi.org/10.1037/0033-2909.124.2.240.

34. Shah, Anuj K., Sendhil Mullainathan, and Eldar Shafir. "Some Consequences of Having Too Little." *Science* 338, no. 6107 (2012): 682–685. https://doi.org/10.1126/science.1222426.

35. Mani, Anandi, Sendhil Mullainathan, Eldar Shafir, and Jiaying Zhao. "Poverty Impedes Cognitive Function." *Science* 341, no. 6149 (2013): 976–980. https://doi.org/10.1126/science.1238041.

36. Swee, Michael B., Kelsey Klein, Shannon Murray, and Richard G. Heimberg. "A Brief Self-Compassionate Letter-Writing Intervention for Individuals with High Shame." *Mindfulness* 14, no. 4 (2023): 854–867. https://doi.org/10.1007/s12671-023-02097-5.

37. Oyserman, Daphna, and Mesmin Destin. "Identity-Based Motivation: Implications for Intervention." *The Counseling Psychologist* 38, no. 7 (2010): 1001–1043. https://doi.org/10.1177/0011000010374775.

38. Wood, Wendy, and David T. Neal. "A New Look at Habits and the Habit-Goal Interface." *Psychological Review* 114, no. 4 (2007): 843–863. https://doi.org/10.1037/0033-295X.114.4.843.

39. Samuelson, William, and Richard Zeckhauser. "Status Quo Bias in Decision Making." *Journal of Risk and Uncertainty* 1 (1988): 7–59. https://doi.org/10.1007/BF00055564.

END NOTES

40. Prochaska, James O., Wayne F. Velicer, Joseph S. Rossi, Michael G. Goldstein, Brian H. Marcus, William Rakowski, et al. "Stages of Change and Decisional Balance for 12 Problem Behaviors." *Health Psychology* 13, no. 1 (1994): 39–46. https://doi.org/10.1037/0278-6133.13.1.39.

41. Holt-Lunstad, Julianne, Timothy B. Smith, and J. Bradley Layton. "Social Relationships and Mortality Risk: A Meta-Analytic Review." *PLOS Medicine* 7, no. 7 (2010): e1000316. https://doi.org/10.1371/journal.pmed.1000316.

42. Collins, N. L., and B. C. Feeney. "A Safe Haven: An Attachment Theory Perspective on Support Seeking and Caregiving in Intimate Relationships." *Journal of Personality and Social Psychology* 78, no. 6 (2000): 1053–1073. https://doi.org/10.1037/0022-3514.78.6.1053.

43. Edmondson, A. "Psychological Safety and Learning Behavior in Work Teams." *Administrative Science Quarterly* 44, no. 2 (1999): 350–383. https://doi.org/10.2307/2666999.

44. López-Castro, T., et al. "Association Between Shame and Posttraumatic Stress Disorder: A Meta-Analysis." *Journal of Traumatic Stress* 32, no. 4 (2019): 484–495. https://doi.org/10.1002/jts.22411.

45. Orchowski, L. M., A. S. Untied, and C. A. Gidycz. "Social Reactions to Disclosure of Sexual Victimization and Adjustment among Survivors of Sexual Assault." *Journal of Interpersonal Violence* 28, no. 10 (2013): 2005–2023. https://doi.org/10.1177/0886260512471085.

46. Littleton, H. L. "The Impact of Social Support and Negative Disclosure Reactions on Sexual Assault Victims: A Cross-Sectional and Longitudinal Investigation." *Journal of Trauma*

& *Dissociation* 11, no. 2 (2010): 210–227. https://doi.org/10.1080/15299730903502946.

47. Frattaroli, J. "Experimental Disclosure and Its Moderators: A Meta-Analysis." *Psychological Bulletin* 132, no. 6 (2006): 823–865. https://doi.org/10.1037/0033-2909.132.6.823.

48. Au, T. M., S. Sauer-Zavala, M. W. King, N. Petrocchi, D. H. Barlow, and B. T. Litz. "Compassion-Based Therapy for Trauma-Related Shame and Posttraumatic Stress: Initial Evaluation Using a Multiple Baseline Design." *Behavior Therapy* 48, no. 2 (2017): 207–221. https://doi.org/10.1016/j.beth.2016.11.012.

ACKNOWLEDGMENTS

My Appreciation to You

"Our greatest strength isn't in the opinions of others; it lies in our own." –Keyimani Alford

First, I want to thank everyone who has believed in my potential—those who believed I could write something meaningful and trusted that my words could matter. In a world filled with millions of books, you chose *this* one. That choice is not lost on me.

I don't call you fans. I call you family. Family invests in each other. And because you have invested in me—your time, your attention, your encouragement—I want you to know how grateful I am. Without you, I wouldn't be able to do what I do or continue to pour purpose back into the lives of others. This book exists because of you.

You've also given me space to reflect—on opinions, on criticism, on kindness, and on the full spectrum of how people show up in the world. Your passion, your support, your love, and even your honest feedback—whether positive or critical—helped shape this work. I wanted to create something that could support us as we navigate life, especially in moments that cause mental strain and uncertainty about what comes next.

I wrote this book for you. And I wrote it for me.

Think. Speak. Manifest.

To the experts, philosophers, and professionals who may read this and wonder whether I'm "too much" or "a little different"—thank you. You're not wrong. I've spent years suppressing parts of myself to fit expectations and keep peace. But I've learned that when you get free from the need for approval, you unlock clarity, courage, and purpose. Without that freedom, this book would not exist.

To my friends, my closest friends, and my family—thank you for listening. Thank you for the late conversations, the questions, the curiosity, and even the disagreements. Thank you for engaging with my ideas instead of dismissing them. That kind of dialogue is a gift, and I don't take it lightly.

To God—thank You. I trust that You are intentional in all You do, and I am grateful for the purpose You've placed within me and the opportunity to walk it out. This work is part of that calling.

And to my colleagues and those who have trusted me with their platforms, classrooms, stages, and spaces—thank you. Thank you for believing in this message and allowing me to give language to experiences many of us struggle to articulate.

Every part of this journey matters to me.

Thank you—for reading, for reflecting, and for being here.

THE AUTHOR

About Keyimani Alford

Keyimani L. Alford is an award-winning author, Amazon bestselling writer, speaker, and the founder of Keywords Unlocked Publishers, a minority-owned publishing company dedicated to helping writers turn their ideas and lived experiences into professional, impactful books. Through his work, Dr. Alford has helped amplify voices, especially those from underrepresented communities, guiding authors to tell their stories with clarity, confidence, and authenticity.

At the heart of Dr. Alford's work is one mission: to help people reclaim control of their inner narrative so they can live, lead, and create with intention. His writing challenges readers to confront the thought patterns that quietly shape their decisions, relationships, and sense of self—while offering practical tools to move forward with courage and purpose.

While higher education has been a significant part of his professional journey, Dr. Alford's identity extends far beyond titles and institutions. He is someone who values real conversation, personal growth, and the freedom that comes from self-awareness. He believes transformation begins when people stop performing for approval and start living in alignment with who they were created to be.

Think. Speak. Manifest.

Outside of his professional work, Dr. Alford enjoys traveling, spending time outdoors, and unwinding with a good horror movie. He finds inspiration in new environments, honest dialogue, and moments that invite reflection. Whether on the page or on a stage, his voice is rooted in hope, truth, and the belief that every person has the capacity to rewrite their story.

Dr. Alford's work exists to remind people that their thoughts matter, their voice carries weight, and their purpose is worth pursuing—fully and unapologetically.

How to Stay in Touch with Me

If this book spoke to you, I'd love to stay connected. Here are the best ways to keep growing with me beyond these pages:

1. **Join the Newsletter (Reflection Corner)**
   Short encouragement, mindset tools, and practical reflection prompts you can use in real life—especially when your mind starts getting loud.
   https://drkeyspeaks.com/about-drkey/

2. **Watch on YouTube**
   I share motivation, inspiration, and honest conversations about the things we all face—fear, pressure, purpose, identity, and the mental patterns that try to keep us stuck. Subscribe: www.youtube.com/@drkeyspeaks

3. **Connect on Social**
   Daily reminders, mindset shifts, and moments that help you stay anchored.
   - Facebook | Instagram |drkeyspeaks

4. **Speaking + Blog + Updates**
   For blog posts, resources, and invitations to book me for conferences, events, and leadership spaces: drkeyspeaks.com

Learn more and access everything in one place: *@drkeyspeaks*

Think it. Speak it. Manifest it.

Leave a Review

Thank you for reading Think. Speak. Manifest. If this book helped you, would you take a moment to leave an honest review?

Reviews help other readers find the book, and they help authors keep going.

Scan the QR code to review on Amazon.

Prefer to type it instead?
https://a.co/d/0gr0kAXl

Thank you for supporting my work.

Think it. Speak it. Manifest it.

Thank you for your support. We hope you enjoyed this Keywords Unlocked Publishers book.

Keywords Unlocked Publishers® is a minority-owned publishing company founded by Dr. Keyimani Alford to help writers tell their stories with purpose and professionalism—without losing their creative control.

We support aspiring and established authors with services such as:

Author consulting
for clarifying your vision and publishing next steps

Professional interior layout
for print and eBook formats

Manuscript guidance
for market-ready presentation, formatting, and publishing

If you'd like more information about our services, resources, and publishing support, contact us:

Keywords Unlocked Publishers®
6969 N. Port Washington Road, Suite B150, PMB 1025
Glendale, WI 53217
608-957-7233
keywordsunlockedllc@gmail.com
keywordsunlocked.com
Your voice. Your story. Unlocked.